GREAT COACHING
IDEAS

Dr Peter Shaw

Marshall Cavendish
Business

1 New Industrial Road, Singapore 536196
genrefsales@sg.marshallcavendish.com
www.marshallcavendish.com/genref

Other Marshall Cavendish offices: Marshall Cavendish Corporation. 99 White Plains Road, Tarrytown NY 10591-9001, USA • Marshall Cavendish International (Thailand) Co Ltd. 253 Asoke, 12th Flr, Sukhumvit 21 Road, Klongtoey Nua, Wattana, Bangkok 10110, Thailand • Marshall Cavendish (Malaysia) Sdn Bhd, Times Subang, Lot 46, Subang Hi-Tech Industrial Park, Batu Tiga, 40000 Shah Alam, Selangor Darul Ehsan, Malaysia

Marshall Cavendish is a trademark of Times Publishing Limited

National Library Board, Singapore Cataloguing-in-Publication Data
Shaw, Peter.
100 great coaching ideas / Dr Peter Shaw. — Singapore : Marshall Cavendish Business, 2014.
pages cm.
ISBN: 978-981-4516-05-1 (paperback)
1. Employees—Coaching of. 2. Employees—Training of. 3. Mentoring in business.
I. Title. II. One hundred great coaching ideas.
HF5549.5.C53
658.3124—dc23   OCN858526260

Printed and bound by CPI Group (UK) Ltd, Croydon, CR0 4YY

This book is dedicated to my coaching colleagues at

Praesta Partners whom I work most closely:

Barry Woledge, James Thorne, Steve Wigzell, Ian Angell,

Hilary Douglas and Paul Gray. They are a delight to work with

and always bring new ideas and approaches.

TITLES IN THE **100 GREAT IDEAS** SERIES

100 Great Branding Ideas by Sarah McCartney

100 Great Business Ideas by Jeremy Kourdi

100 Great Business Leaders by Jonathan Gifford

100 Great Coaching Ideas by Peter Shaw

100 Great Copywriting Ideas by Andy Maslen

100 Great Cost-cutting Ideas by Anne Hawkins

100 Great Innovation Ideas by Howard Wright

100 Great Leadership Ideas by Jonathan Gifford

100 More Great Leadership Ideas by Jonathan Gifford

100 Great Marketing Ideas by Jim Blythe

100 Great Personal Impact Ideas by Peter Shaw

100 Great PR Ideas by Jim Blythe

100 Great Presentation Ideas by Patrick Forsyth

100 Great Sales Ideas by Patrick Forsyth

100 Great Time Management Ideas by Patrick Forsyth

CONTENTS

Acknowledgements   xi
Foreword by Charlie Massey   xiii
Introduction   xvi

DEVELOPING YOUR COACHING SKILLS
Section A: The Approach   I

1   See questions as keys that unlock   2
2   Leave space for reflection   4
3   Bring a focus on facts   6
4   Bring clarity about the organisation's objectives   8
5   Be realistic about possibilities   10
6   Understand the motivations   12
7   Listen to the emotions   14
8   Trust your intuition   16
9   Allow for rational and emotional reactions   18
10 Bring insights and not solutions   21

Section B: The Practicalities   23

11 The agenda   24
12 Pace the conversation   26
13 Be adaptable   28
14 Be responsive   30
15 Be clear on the time available   32
16 Reach agreement on next steps   34
17 Choose the frequency and location of conversations   36
18 Ensure a review of an individual's progress   38
19 See each conversation as part of a journey   40
20 Use short, focused conversations well   42

Section C: The Coaching Conversations 44

21 Balance the longer term and the shorter term 45
22 Recognise how individuals learn 47
23 Enable someone to live their values 49
24 Ensure harsh reality is faced up to 51
25 Seek feedback on what has worked 53
26 Review the outcomes after a period 55
27 Be mindful of the individual's energy levels 57
28 Use yourself as a barometer 59
29 Allow someone to find their own way to solve a problem 61
30 Bring respect for the individual's experience
and qualities 63
31 Ensure pitfalls and risks are understood 66
32 Believe that good can come out of any situation 68
33 Walk alongside someone at a measured distance 70
34 Allow for silence and quietness 72
35 Enable an individual to draw from their own experience 74
36 Celebrate progress 76
37 Enable individuals to crystallize their learning 78
38 Encourage contributions within wider teams 80
39 Create mutual support structures 82
40 Reinforce independence of mind and spirit 84

Section D: Your Own Learning about Coaching 85

41 Keep reviewing your learning 86
42 Develop your thinking with trusted others 88
43 Work in partnership with others 90
44 Recognise when specialist help is needed 92
45 Know your limitations 95
46 Use an external business coach wisely 97
47 Understand your own emotions 100
48 Recognise when your job is done 102

49   Celebrate your own journey as a coach   104
50   Look forward with expectation   106

APPLYING COACHING IN SPECIFIC CONTEXTS
Section E: Ensuring High Quality Outcomes   108

51   Creating bold expectations about outcomes   109
52   Building a pathway to success   111
53   Fostering an awareness of risks   113
54   Knowing how progress will be measured   115
55   Bringing clarity of role   118

Section F: Enabling Someone to Step up in Responsibility   120

56   Creating a picture of success   121
57   Drawing from previous steps   123
58   Building on strengths   125
59   Recognising what 'being grown up' means   127
60   Taking bigger strides   129

Section G: Building Strong Partnerships   131

61   Recognising shared interests   132
62   Building common purpose   134
63   Knowing where your fixed points are   136
64   Having honest conversations on progress   138
65   Dealing effectively with differences   140

Section H: Leading Change Well   142

66   Building acceptance about the need for change   143
67   Creating a shared vision about desired outcomes   146
68   Building champions   148
69   Ensuring a balance between realism and optimism   150
70   Keeping both focus and adaptability   152

Section I: Growing an Individual with Potential   154

71 Encouraging belief in what is possible   155
72 Bringing frankness about necessary development   157
73 Creating stretching situations   160
74 Ensuring clear feedback   163
75 Ensuring clear but not excessive expectations   166

Section J: Managing Someone with Limitations   169

76 Ensuring an objective perspective   170
77 Understanding an individual's characteristics
        and emotions   172
78 Having an honest conversation   175
79 Building clarity about options going forward   178
80 Making hard decisions   180

Section K: Building Effective Teams   183

81 Seeing the potential   184
82 Create time for reflection   187
83 Recognising corporate leadership responsibility   189
84 Role modelling partnership working   192
85 Drawing out each other's capabilities   194

Section L: Building Motivation in an Organisation   197

86 Recognising the signalling effect of the leader   198
87 Knowing how to generate energy   201
88 Nurturing curiosity and innovation   203
89 Building hope and expectation about possibilities   205
90 Ensuring consistent behaviour   209

Section M: Developing Resilience and Adaptability   210

91   Understanding the effects of the individual's
         recent history   211
92   Knowing the emotional pressure points   214
93   Growing personal resilience   216
94   Developing agility and adaptability   218
95   Keeping fit in body, mind and spirit   220

Section N: Enabling an Openness to Change   220

96   Seeing life as an exploration   223
97   Keeping the balance between fixed points and
         new insights   225
98   Allowing learning to be never ending   228
99   Believing the impossible is possible   230
100 Enabling love to conquer fear   232

Books by Dr Peter Shaw   234
About the Author   236

ACKNOWLEDGEMENTS

THIS BOOK IS dedicated to the coaches I work most closely with at Praesta Partners. I thoroughly enjoy working with my colleague partners, Ian Angel, Barry Woledge, Steve Wigzell and James Thorne, as well as with Paul Gray and Hilary Douglas who are my two other colleagues in the public sector cluster. It has always been very stimulating to talk with those gifted individuals about the leadership challenges our clients face and the most appropriate coaching approaches to apply in different situations.

I have been coaching for ten years and have had the pleasure of working with a wide range of delightful clients from many different sectors in different countries. I owe them all a debt of gratitude for enabling me to share in their journeys. I enjoy the coaching work even more year on year with no desire to retire.

Jackie Tookey has typed this manuscript with immense patience. Jackie has been an important encouragement to me as I have written this book. Sonia John-Lewis has organised my diary with great skill and has kept me focused in my use of time. I am grateful to Anthony Hopkins for his practical advice in enabling the business of Praesta Partners to run smoothly. Melvin Neo has been an admirable editor giving me the opportunity to put this book together. I am grateful to Charlie Massey for writing the foreword to the book. Charlie has been a great encouragement to me over the 10 years we have known each other.

This book was written over the summer of 2013 in Godalming, Harlesdon and Lochalsh. This variety of settings of the Surrey countryside, inner city London and the Scottish mountains has enabled me to think about how coaching can be applied in different ways with very different people. Throughout the time when I have been writing this book my wife, Frances has shown immense patience and has been wonderfully supportive.

ACKNOWLEDGEMENTS

FOREWORD

The best leaders and coaches, whether consciously or not, help lift people's sights to see what they can be, not just what they are.

Over the years I have had the great privilege of working with an enormous number of talented people in my different leadership roles working with and within Government, the wider public sector, the voluntary sector, and the private sector. On many occasions I have found the talent of those around me to be quite daunting. But as I stepped into bigger and wider roles I realised that I could no longer rely on my own skills to solve every problem that came my way, and that I needed to rely increasingly on unlocking the excellence of those people around me to ensure that we were able to succeed.

This realisation hit me with most force in the early years of the millennium, when I led teams in the Prime Minister's Strategy Unit working firstly on childcare strategy and then on drugs policy. It was with enormous relief that I realised that it was not my job to have all the answers. Instead, a core part of my role was to understand the strengths of the team around me, ask the right questions, and bring fresh perspectives to the most intractable issues that we needed to work through. Whilst I did at times feel very humbled (and at times rather fraudulent) to lead such capable individuals and teams to successful outcomes, I also felt enormous pride in seeing them move on to greater achievements themselves, with increased confidence in what they could do.

As I reflect on those times and all of the great people I have led, I have come to the view that being a great coach requires a strong dose of humanity in really caring about, and believing in, your people. For them to see the extent of their potential, you need to believe it and then commit to work with them to unlock it. Succeeding in doing that can be one of the most rewarding things you can do as a leader. For me, seeing people blossom and develop and move on to bigger and better roles has been a great source of energy and pride, as well as an enormous privilege.

I have been very lucky to have worked with Peter for over ten years. During that time, I have been fortunate enough to have reached leadership roles that I would have found difficult to believe possible when we started working together. When I reflect on that time, and on Peter's strengths, I am struck by Peter's skill in asking me the right questions that have allowed me to reflect on and embed my learning from the different experiences I have had. And as I have moved into more senior and complex roles, Peter has helped me to reflect on the particular value that I add in any given situation and what it is that only I can do.

An important element of Peter's book is the notion that whilst we all need to be aware of our limitations, every leader should try to develop a suite of coaching skills to get the most out of their people, for example in helping staff new to the organisation or role understand the context of their role, and to assimilate new cultures effectively and quickly. It is not something that should therefore be seen as the sole preserve of externally procured support. The complimentary stimulus from the external coach can then be to bring valuable wider expertise and perspective, and to equip the leader to coach their people effectively.

Regardless of your field or expertise, I hope that you will find this book to be a really useful source of ideas as you reflect and build on your skills as a coach. Peter has structured it in a way that should allow you to dip in and out of it, using the different sections as prompts for thought. I also hope that it will help you to reflect on the importance of this element of your role – developing and applying your coaching skills should be one of the most enjoyable parts of leadership, as you see teams and individuals fulfil their potential.

Charlie Massey
Director General, Strategy and External Relations
Department of Health
London, England

INTRODUCTION

THIS BOOK IS written for managers and leaders at any level, in any organisation, in any country. The book will provide you with a quarry of ideas and prompts for thought.

The good manager or leader is focused on bringing the best out of their people. A crucial skill is to be able to use a coaching approach effectively to draw out the experience and capabilities of those working for you and with you. In a fast-moving world coaching skills are an essential pre-requisite of good leadership and management. They are not an optional extra.

The good manager wants to catch the imagination of individuals and teams so that they see what is possible and are motivated to have a significant impact. The good leader who brings the best out of their people will use a range of coaching approaches and will focus their use on members of their staff when they are facing transition or needing to step up to new challenges and demands.

This book is deliberately split into two halves. The first half is about developing your coaching skills. It looks at your approach, the practicalities, the coaching conversations and your own learning about coaching. One way of using the book is to reflect each day on one particular skill and see how it can be used and developed. Then you will have the pleasure of using them in combination and begin to see some of the positive benefits.

The second half looks at ten different contexts where coaching skills can be applied to good effect to enable individuals and teams to reach practical outcomes. The ten contexts are:

- Ensuring high quality outcomes

- Enabling someone to step up in responsibility

- Building strong partnerships

- Leading change well

- Growing an individual with potential

- Managing someone with limitations

- Building effective teams

- Building motivation in an organisation

- Developing resilience and adaptability

- Enabling an openness to change

Using coaching approaches well depends on you as a manager being willing to stand back and not always be in direct control. You need the capacity to reflect on your own approach and to be willing to be adaptable. Success comes through enabling others to review and reframe, and to be refocused and re-energised.

Using a coaching approach can be a liberating experience. It will release you from feeling you have to solve every problem yourself. Applying a coaching approach is just as demanding, but in a very different way. Your ability to ask the right question and bring different insights becomes much more important than finding an instant solution.

The manager who coaches well is able to conserve their mental, emotional and physical energy so it can be deployed when it can be at its most effective. Developing coaching skills often sits alongside an individual becoming increasingly clear in their understanding of where they can make a distinctive contribution. Bringing out the best in others will enable you to bring out the best in yourself as it becomes clearer, 'what is it only you can do to ensure the success of the particular endeavour?'

In workshops I lead I often ask people to work in pairs where they coach each other for periods of five minutes. This use of short, focused coaching has persuaded me that most people have the ability to use coaching skills as part of their management repertoire. Hence the belief that a practical book with 100 ideas could provide a valuable tool for managers and leaders at any level, in any organisation, in any country.

I have drawn from my first career of working in the public sector for 32 years and then a second career working in the private sector for 10 years, alongside a number of roles within the voluntary sector. I hope the ideas in the book provide valuable prompts for thought and action. Enjoy developing and using coaching skills. It will give you immense satisfaction to see people responding and having a far bigger impact than they had ever thought possible.

Dr Peter Shaw
Godalming, Surrey, United Kingdom
peter.shaw@praesta.com

PART 1

DEVELOPING YOUR COACHING SKILLS

THE APPROACH

1 SEE QUESTIONS AS KEYS THAT UNLOCK

FINDING THE RIGHT question can be more important than identifying the solution.

The idea

The effective leader as coach is not telling people the solution to every problem. You may be bringing insights and the benefit of past experiences, but the most important contribution you can make is to ask pertinent questions and enable individuals and teams to think through possibilities and reach their own conclusions.

The good question challenges, enables and empowers. Providing the solution may not energise, enable or empower. As a leader you want successful outcomes to be reached and your people to grow in confidence and competence. You want to see individuals finding their own solutions having been prompted through good questions.

The best questions are open-ended such as, "What are the opportunities?", "What can we learn from others?", "What type of options do we need to explore?", "What are the potential blockages we need to examine further?" and, "What are the next steps which can be taken?"

If you think your role is always to provide solutions you will become exhausted and not have a particularly motivated group of people working with you. If you see your task as asking good, open-ended questions, you will be liberated from the belief that you have to solve every problem yourself.

Katherine was a newly promoted head of department in a college. She had lots of ideas about turning around her department. She knew she had to keep her enthusiasm under control and bring the other members of the department along with her.

At an early team meeting she posed the question, "How do we want people to describe our department in six months' time?" This question led to a fruitful discussion out of which Katherine drew out priorities for the department. These priorities were very similar to, but not identical to those she already had in her mind. Using the approach of starting with a question helped build a strong sense of shared energy, and created a better outcome than would have been her initial proposition.

In practice

- See your role as asking the right questions rather than finding the solutions

- Observe how others use questions well and adopt their best practice

- Observe how different people respond to different types of questions

- Construct questions which open up discussion and enable possibilities to be identified

- Spend time thinking through the right questions and give space for them to be addressed

LEAVE SPACE FOR REFLECTION

Leaving some space for reflection is essential in order to reach outcomes that are sustainable. The amount of reflection needed will vary by individual and team.

The idea

The corollary of asking a good question is allowing space for reflection. What we often observe is, 'more haste and less speed'. Without reflection decisions can be rushed and ill-thought through, with side consequences that had not been anticipated. The rushed decision is often regretted and reversed.

Ensuring space for reflection can be about the way meetings are paced, so that there is time for a variety of angles to be considered. What might be needed is space for reflection between meetings so that evidence can be considered and opinions sought.

Space for reflection might mean returning to a subject the following day. It might mean letting our subconscious do its thinking overnight so we end up with a more balanced perspective and a clearer resolve about what is the most appropriate way forward.

For some, the space needed for reflection is a quiet place where issues are processed internally and quietly. For others what is needed is the opportunity to talk issues through with reflection happening through dialogue rather than silence.

It helps if you understand how each of your key people reflect and reach conclusions, and have a view about how best can you work with them so that their means of reflection is respected and enabled.

Katherine had two deputy departmental leaders. Katherine knew that Michael's preference was to talk issues through whereas Nicky's preference was to reflect quietly on different possibilities. Katherine invited them to share their preferences about how they reflect.

Katherine invited them to work through some examples of issues they would need to address as a means of working through in advance how they were going to consider these issues and ensure practical solutions. They were, therefore, able to agree in advance the type of reflection they wanted to include as a team and as individuals. This agreement was helpful in planning the way forward.

In practice

- Be open about how you best reflect and what you need from others to reflect constructively

- Allow time for reflection when decisions need to be made

- Encourage open conversation about what type of reflection works best for each member of the team

- Allow opportunities for the subconscious mind to do the thinking before a final decision is made

- Be mindful of the balance between reflection through dialogue, and reflection through quiet space

BRING A FOCUS ON FACTS

THE DISCIPLINE OF always coming back to "what are the facts?" can ensure that decisions and action are always based on reality rather than myth.

The idea

The boring recognition of the question, "what are the facts that matter?" can help ground a discussion and the consideration of future options. The facts may be about data and resources, and about opinions and perceptions. Clarity about the evidence is crucial to underpin robustness of any decision-making. Testing the evidence so the facts are clearly robust is a process that needs to be repeated on a regular basis.

Your role as leader might be to ensure that the robustness of data is tested through different perspectives and the drawing in of different types of expertise. Your role might also be to ensure that the wider perspective is understood, so that the facts about the nature of the opposition, or type of opportunities are fully appreciated.

Your role might be to ask questions about, "what are the key facts?", "how is the factual context changing?", "what is the fresh evidence that is likely to be available over the coming weeks?" Your role might be to be persistent in stressing what information should be in place before a final decision is taken. You might be able to build links with different organisations or people who can provide new relevant information and insight. Progress can come from pointing people in the right direction so they collect the right type of data going forward.

There were different views in Katherine's team about what should be the focus of the curriculum over the forthcoming academic year. Katherine sensed that personal preference and people's prior knowledge were playing too big a part. Katherine suggested that more evidence was needed about the views of current students on what had worked well, plus evidence from prospective students about what type of curriculum offerings would catch their imagination.

Katherine recognised that the data they collected could only be partial, but without some more facts about people's experiences and preferences they could not move forward to a more considered conclusion. The facts they put together about the experiences of present students and the preferences of prospective students enabled them to reach agreement about decisions going forward and provided a clear basis for next steps.

In practice

- See facts as covering both data and the perspectives of different interest groups

- Be relentless about the importance of focusing on key facts

- Encourage a pro-active approach to gleaning new evidence

- Ensure a focus on key facts and be observant about whether individuals are becoming overwhelmed by a mass of data

- Be mindful of the emotional reaction against uncomfortable facts

BRING CLARITY ABOUT THE ORGANISATION'S OBJECTIVES

BRINGING AS MUCH clarity as possible about an organisation's objectives will provide an important context within which individuals and teams develop their own particular next steps.

The idea

Whatever level you are at in an organisation you can bring a wider understanding of the context than the people who work for you. This understanding is in your head. You may think the context is perfectly obvious: it might be to you, but not for people who are less senior than you. You are present at meetings that they are not part of. You see, hear and read things that give you greater clarity than those who are more focused on specific and detailed issues.

Your role as leader is to ensure that the organisation's objectives are communicated clearly and simply so that they are remembered and acted upon. Sometimes this is about formal, written objectives. At other times it is your interpreting what you hear from above and outside, so you are up-dating in an intelligible way those working in your area of the business.

When events are moving quickly because the market is changing, or finances have become difficult, you have a responsibility to bring as much clarity as possible so that people who look to you, understand what they need to know. Sometimes absolute clarity is not possible, but admitting the uncertainties and then bringing as reasonable a degree of clarity as possible can give people the reassurance which enables them to focus on doing the best possible job they can.

The college where Katherine was head of department emphasized its record in getting its students into top universities. There appeared to be an overriding objective to increase the numbers going to the best UK universities. The detailed objectives for the college referred to a range of different avenues including employment as well as higher education.

Katherine worked with the team in her department to ensure they were clear that what mattered was bringing clarity about a range of different, potential options for students and enabling them to make the most informed choices about their next steps. Katherine's senior team recognised the importance of the rhetoric about top level higher education places, but ensured their own activity was focused around a wider range of good outcomes.

In practice

- Articulate the objectives of the organisation simply, clearly and often

- Keep updating those objectives in the light of the market, and financial and political changes

- Use a variety of means to communicate the objectives orally and in writing

- Keep checking that the organisation's objectives are understood by people working for you

- Use examples that bring the objectives alive and demonstrate their importance

5 **BE REALISTIC ABOUT POSSIBILITIES**

SHAPING POSSIBILITIES AND describing them in a realistic, attractive and attainable way is central to building a sense of shared exploration and common purpose.

The idea

Your role as leader is often to describe the wider context, draw out the objectives and identify the broad way forward. You are creating a framework within which others are working. It is like painting the broad landscape within which more detailed work is done by others.

As a leader who coaches you are shaping and steering rather than doing and rowing. In the process of shaping you are likely to be drawing out possibilities for further consideration. Part of your task might include describing the fixed points about what is possible and where progress ought to be deliverable.

Your role might be to set out two or three possible routes to a destination allowing your team to think through the detailed pros and cons and with your team then recommending what might be the most appropriate way forward.

As ideas are developed, part of your role might be to bring a perspective about where barriers are likely to impede progress and how they might be overcome. You may need to combine both inspiring and encouraging people to think through new and different approaches, and bring a sense of realism about barriers and how they might be overcome.

Katherine wanted to enhance the reputation of her department within the college. She talked with her team about how they might build the department's reputation with a range of different schools. They came up with a mix of ideas about partnerships, shadowing and exchanges. Katherine welcomed the wealth of ideas.

Katherine saw her role as bringing tempered realism, but not in a way that stifled creative thinking. The team ended up with a clear plan with three main priorities. Katherine felt she had shaped the conversation without dominating it. The consequence was that all members of the department were committed to a range of outreach activities.

In practice

- See your role as shaping and steering rather than doing and directing

- Encourage a wide-range of possibilities to be examined

- Bring a sense of realism without stifling creative conversation

- Be mindful when you limit the possibilities to a manageable number so it is neither too early nor too late in the process

- Congratulate people for developing possibilities before diluting their expectations through bringing in a dose of realism

UNDERSTAND THE MOTIVATIONS

BRINGING THE BEST out of your people means understanding both their competences and their values and motivations.

The idea

When you seek to recruit someone, their CV sets out their qualifications and experience which enables you to build a picture of the type of contribution that they can make within your organisation.

You can fairly rapidly build up an initial perspective about their competences and practical expertise. But what matters more than experience and competence are values and motivations. You want to know if someone will be a member of the team who is able to operate effectively with others and will bring integrity, and has values that are aligned with those of the team. As you understand someone's motivation for joining your organisation you can begin to appreciate the type of contribution they will make and the impact they are going to have on their colleagues.

The leader who understands the motivations of their people is going to be in the best possible position to coach them successfully. Understanding motivations can enable you to assist someone to build on their sense of ambition, and their desire to make a difference, or deliver a specific outcome that they are passionate about achieving. Sometimes the good leader as coach is helping someone to temper their motivations so they are more realistic and are steered in a way that is less likely to lead to disappointment.

Henry was the managing partner of a small accountancy firm with a well-qualified group of partners and staff. Henry knew their technical competences well and recognised the wealth of expertise he had at his disposal, but he recognised he needed to understand better the motivations of the individual partners.

Henry had a one-to-one conversation with each of them seeking to build up a clearer understanding about their personal priorities and what motivated them to come to work. Henry was surprised about what he learnt. He realised that he had taken his colleagues for granted over a number of years and had not refreshed his understanding about their changing motivations.

In practice

- See motivations as just as important as competences

- Keep up to date about the evolving motivations that different individuals bring to their work

- Seek to understand the underlying values which lead to the motivations you observe in others

- Recognise when some motivations can be destructive if they are primarily about personal ambition

- Seek to enable people to understand how others see their motivations and to recognise when that perception can have a negative effect

LISTEN TO THE EMOTIONS

It can be helpful to seek to listen to the emotions behind the words and to observe the interplay of emotions as well as the verbal dialogue.

The idea

Data is transmitted all the time through emotions. We are affected by the emotions of others much more quickly than we realise. Sometimes our own emotional reactions catapult us into using a sequence of words that we had not pre-planned. The emotional interchange is often faster and much more unpredictable than the words.

Sometimes it can be helpful to pose the explicit question to yourself, "what are the emotions I am observing and what are they telling me?" Sometimes when an individual is arguing a particular case and looks frustrated it can be an emotion that derives from a different event which is dominating their perspective. Grief in someone's personal life, or frustration in a different element of an individual's work, can spill over into an emotional reaction in a debate that is taking place or in a decision that needs to be made.

Emotional noise from other areas of someone's life can readily contaminate their thinking. When we know the issues someone is addressing across the full range of their work and life we can more readily, in listening to their emotions, differentiate between emotional baggage and good insights that come through the perspective of their emotions.

Henry knew there was some unhappiness amongst a group of the partners. He was not quite sure how much of this was substantive and how much resulted from frustration outside work. He was conscious that one person was having to manage a very difficult teenager, while another was handling two parents with dementia, while a third partner was in financial difficulties following a divorce. Another partner had been unsuccessful in an application to become the senior partner of another business.

Henry talked individually with each of the partners to understand what was fulfilling or frustrating about their work, and to understand the wider perspective from their personal lives. In these discussions he listened to their emotions and was able to assess the extent to which their emotions were limiting their effectiveness at work. Henry sought to help each individual prioritise their work and energy. Henry was sympathetic to their personal circumstances without it leading to treating them in an over sympathetic way.

In practice

- Listen carefully to the emotions as well as the words

- Take time to understand the reasons for emotional reactions

- Be mindful where emotional reactions are contaminating someone's judgement

- Be sympathetic when there are external factors leading to difficult emotional situations, whilst keeping an independent and objective perspective

- Recognise when your own emotions come into play and listen to what your emotions are telling you about what is going on in a particular situation

8 TRUST YOUR INTUITION

YOUR INTUITION IS based on your experience and values and is always giving you valuable perspectives, which need to be tested to be sure they are robust.

The idea

We can readily dismiss our intuitive sense as irrational and emotive. But our intuitive perspective often brings valuable insight. When we meet someone for the first time we decide instinctively whether we trust them and how we are going to react to them. First impressions may not be accurate, but often give us valuable, initial data which it is right to test over time.

In any new situation we are relying on our intuition. As a problem is presented to us we will have an initial set of propositions in our mind about how we handle that issue. As a problem is brought to us by a member of staff our first reaction might be to think of a solution that has worked in the past in a similar context. This example may be the right thing to share, or it might be right to use a sequence of questions that enables someone to work through their own answers to this problem.

Sometimes using our intuition is about trying out different approaches and seeing what works with different individuals. Sometimes your intuitive sense might be to use a story to help someone see an issue from another angle. On other occasions you might want to drop in a particular thought or idea or you might ask a question about what might or might not work going forward, or we might invite them to draw from their previous experience to see if there are any parallels that might inform next steps.

Trusting your intuition is not about acting randomly. It is about using patterns that have worked well before and adapting them to fit individual circumstances. It is recognising what works well with different people and then adapting approaches to suit different circumstances.

When Henry was presented with a proposal by a couple of the partners for expanding the business in a specific area, he had an intuitive sense that this idea would not work. Henry decided not to be negative about the idea at the start. He posed a sequence of questions about what was the evidence of likely success and how might it affect the rest of the business. He got the two partners to explore ideas further and then set up discussions with a wider group of partners so that the hypothesis could be tested. Gradually the ideas put forward by the two partners began to change shape informed by the views of colleagues. Henry felt the revised formulation was much more likely to be successful. Intuitively he felt much more positive about the likely outcome.

In practice

- Reflect on what your intuition is telling you

- Test your intuition alongside the views of others

- Be open about your intuitive sense and allow others to explore what might be the implications

- Encourage others to share their intuitive reactions and then test them out

- See intuition as providing valuable insights which should not be dismissed lightly

ALLOW FOR RATIONAL AND EMOTIONAL REACTIONS

EACH PERSON BRINGS a mixture of rational and emotional reactions. We need to allow for both in the way we coach individuals and teams.

The idea

Each of us is conscious that we bring a mix of emotional and rational reactions to any situation. Sometimes the emotional reaction is dominant, on other occasions it is the rational brain that overrides. Often the emotional reaction kicks in much more quickly than the rational reaction and time is needed to let our rational reactions catch up with our emotional reactions.

Those we lead will bring a mix of emotional and rational reactions to any situation. The make-up of their personality and their previous experience will affect the rational and emotional reactions in their interaction with each other.

It is possible to identify patterns in particular individuals and to predict when the rational reaction is likely to catch up with the emotional reaction. With some people you know that their emotional reaction has to surface before they will be able to think through the practical next steps. With other people you know that they will be suppressing their emotional reactions and may well need an avenue to let their emotional reactions out before they can move on in their thinking.

If you want to encourage individuals to think about particular longer term priorities, you might want to 'sow some seeds' about possible ways forward so that someone has time to work through their emotional reactions. The gentle comment that, "this approach does not seem to be working as well as we had hoped, perhaps we ought to think about alternative approaches", can be a way of allowing the emotions to work through and then encourage some new thinking about different ways forward.

Henry was conscious that Jane enjoyed working with a particular category of clients but was mindful that the work with this group was beginning to reduce. Henry knew that Jane would need to broaden her portfolio but would be reluctant initially to do so. When Henry began to float the idea that Jane might take on some other clients in a different area of the firm's business he expected a glum look and a lack of enthusiasm.

Henry suggested that he and Jane talk through next steps a couple of weeks later which gave Jane time to work through her emotional reactions. By the time Jane and Henry had the substantive discussion Jane recognised that it was the right decision for her to take on some other clients. She had let her rational thoughts catch up with her initial emotional reaction. She overcame her initial reaction that she had let the firm down because the business from her current clients was declining. She began to feel a sense of excitement about working with new clients and told Henry that she was looking forward to the changes.

In practice

- Allow time for the rational reaction to catch up with the emotional reaction

- Recognise the pattern of interplay in each person between the emotional and rational reaction

- Enable people to have time to process their emotional reactions

- Accept that individuals will have emotional reactions and do not overreact to them

- Ensure individuals see their own pattern of interplay between their rational and emotional reactions

BRING INSIGHTS AND NOT SOLUTIONS

IF YOU CAN bring one clear insight it can help an individual reframe an issue in a way which allows them to move their thinking forward. Often one insight can create a breakthrough.

The idea

One of the Director-Generals in an organisation in which I coached built up a reputation for always bringing a new insight to any situation. If a Director or a Deputy Director was struggling to find a way forward on a particular issue they knew that ten minutes with this trusted and experienced Director-General would lead to a new angle and would often enable them to find a breakthrough. Robert drew from his previous experience in a very skilful way to give a prompt or an example that was memorable. Robert's skill was to enable someone to feel that a problem was solvable and that they could have greater confidence in how they were going to tackle it.

When someone brings an issue to you and wants to talk it through, the right approach is sometimes to focus on the key question. On other occasions sharing an example from your own experience or giving a perspective about what you think is really going on in a particular situation can provide a new angle for an individual looking at what had previously seemed to be an insurmountable problem.

Asking yourself the question, "what is the insight I can bring?" can be a way of using short discussions constructively. If four people want to see you perhaps it is better to have 15 minutes with each person bringing one insight to each person, rather than spending one hour with one person helping to solve their problem for them.

When I lead workshops on subjects ranging from resilience, to leading change well, or being an agile leader, I always ask people at the end what is the key insight they take away. After you have been working with an individual or a team asking the question, "what is the key insight you take away?" can help someone crystallize what is the 'nugget of gold' that they take away from that conversation.

Henry observed that Jim was very determined to build up the business with a particular firm and had a catalogue of reasons why he could make a valuable contribution to this firm. As Jim talked through his next steps Henry was clear that what mattered next was for Jim to build up a good personal relationship with a key decision-maker in this firm.

Henry's insight for Jim was that success would follow from building up the right type of personal relationships that were trusting, respectful and warm. He encouraged Jim to let the facts speak for themselves about the business offering and to put his focus on building up the personal relationships. Jim took away this insight and applied it successfully.

In practice

- Remember those who had brought insights to you and recognise how they did it successfully

- Before a conversation ask yourself, 'what is the insight I can bring?'

- 'Less is more' in terms of leaving someone with one insight to develop rather than a litany of ideas they will not remember

- Encourage someone at the end of a conversation to reflect on 'what is the insight you take away?'

- If time is short your most effective contribution can be to bring one memorable story or one different way of looking at an issue

SECTION B
THE PRACTICALITIES

11 THE AGENDA

AGREEING ON THE agenda for a conversation provides an essential framework but should not be regarded as a straight-jacket.

The idea

As a manager or leader you may want to go into more of a coaching mode in a variety of different conversations and meetings. In addition there may be specific occasions when you are designing a conversation as a coaching conversation.

Where you want to use a coaching approach in a meeting it can be helpful to signal that fact and say that you see your role as asking questions and prompting discussion rather than providing solutions or giving decisions. Flagging up how you intend to handle different items enables others to be in tune with your thinking and approach. Unless you explicitly flag your intent it may take some time for participants to adjust to the different approach you are using.

When it is specifically a coaching conversation there is the opportunity to define the agenda at the start of a single conversation or sequence of conversations. In both cases you have a responsibility to ensure the agenda is manageable and that your approach to the agenda will bring out the best in others.

When it is a coaching conversation, agreeing on an agenda in advance enables someone to think through how they prepare and what they want out of the conversation. Inevitably there may be current issues which it is right to discuss, provided this does not detract from the longer term development objectives which are central to the coaching conversations.

Marilyn was the regional director of a retail chain with an energetic group of senior managers working for her. She set the pace in terms of business targets and chaired purposeful meetings addressing discrete marketing and management issues. She was conscious that her senior managers were happy to do whatever she told them to do but was not convinced that this was the best way forward.

Marilyn wanted her senior managers to step up in their willingness to take responsibility, hence in the business meetings she would sometimes deliberately say that she was going to pose some key questions and get them to work through the solutions. In her one -to-one conversations with her senior managers, Marilyn was clear when she was in directive mode and when she was in coaching mode. She ensured there were discrete discussions about people's development which she always entered in a coaching mode.

In practice

- Be explicit about the agenda and your approach to different items

- Be explicit about when you are in directive mode and when you are in coaching mode

- Vary your style but articulate why you are doing so

- Match your coaching approach to the time available

- Beware lest you slip into directive mode when you have set up coaching-type conversations

12 PACE THE CONVERSATION

How YOU PACE a conversation can be critical to how productive it is.

The idea

When I coach individuals I need to be mindful of the pace that works best for them. For some the most productive conversations are lively and bouncy. I need to be fast-moving with ideas, questions and reflections because that is what stimulates them to be at their most creative and decisive.

For other people the most productive of conversations are slower and more reflective. Often I need to help someone slow down at the start of a coaching conversation so they move from the fast pace which has been essential in their day so far, to a more moderated reflective pace.

There are times when someone has been reflective and it is right to encourage them to up the pace of the crystallizing of their thinking so that they end up with a set of actions they are going to take. Sometimes I up the pace without explicitly checking with the individual because I know the pattern that works well in our conversations. Sometimes I check with the individual whether now is the right moment to up the pace and focus more on next actions.

You will have your own, natural pace that works best for you. You may vary it to an extent in different conversations. You may observe yourself varying your pace depending on the individual, the subject matter, or even the time of day. My encouragement to you is to be mindful about the pace you are taking and to vary that pace deliberately depending on where you want the conversation to go.

A good coaching conversation will often include elements that are more reflective, and then other elements that are more specific and focused. Articulating what you are doing about the pace and why you are varying it can enable someone to respond in a positive way, or deliberately say that they want to take the conversation at a different speed.

Marilyn would often structure her one to ones with her senior managers with the first half being short items where she was passing information or catching up on particular issues, or deciding on next steps on specific issues. Marilyn often used the second half of the meeting for a more reflective conversation on a current issue after flagging up that she was pacing this part of the conversation in a different way.

When Marilyn had one to ones with her senior managers about their own development she paced these conversations more reflectively and then changed gear towards the end when they moved into agreeing some precise, next steps.

In practice

- Observe how you naturally pace different types of conversation

- Be more deliberate in terms of how you manage future conversations

- Be explicit about the type of pace at which you are going to take a conversation

- Observe the natural preferences of others and what helps them either become more reflective, or move more into action mode

- Keep developing your capacity to vary the pace of conversations so you bring out the best in others

13 BE ADAPTABLE

THE ABILITY TO be adaptable increases the likelihood of making progress when the unexpected appears..

The idea

You may have built up a rhythm in the way you work. Your team is responding well to your approach and they are growing in confidence and effectiveness. You are getting plaudits for your style of leadership. But then something goes wrong and your team is in the limelight. You have to be adaptable to the new circumstance and be willing to take accountability for what has happened.

A couple of your team members leave, and the new recruits are very different. You need to think about your approach to leading the team and to bringing out the best in each member of it. Perhaps the financial situation changes and difficult decisions are needed about setting out priorities. You have to adapt your approach and ensure that priorities are crystallized within a few weeks.

In each of these examples your leadership approach needs to change. You have to be adaptable in the way you bring out the best in people. With experienced managers you can steer them gently and ensure there is an effective performance framework. With newly appointed managers you are more committed to mentoring them as they take on their new responsibilities and begin to make an impact. As the new recruits become established you can stand back a bit more and move into a more gentle coaching mode rather than applying a more explicit mentoring-type approach.

Marilyn was conscious that one of her senior managers had recently been recruited from a different retail sector. He brought lots of retail experience but was ingrained in a very different culture. Marilyn saw her role as enabling Bill to do a smooth transition. This meant some fairly tight mentoring initially of Bill about the approaches that worked effectively within the business. At the same time Marilyn did not want to dampen Bill's enthusiasm.

Marilyn wanted to observe his first impressions and use them as valuable data. But she was also conscious that Bill needed steering to help him fit in effectively and be productive quickly. As time went on Marilyn varied her approach with Bill so that it was more of a gentle shaping rather than a direct steering of his approach. Bill was glad of the clear steers of the start, but was then relieved when Marilyn began to stand back and give him the space he wanted to lead his area effectively.

In practice

- Recognise the degree to which you are naturally adaptable or not

- Develop further your adaptability in using different approaches in different contexts

- Recognise that you are able to do both explicit steering and gentle shaping and be mindful about when you adopt these approaches

- Seek feedback about how adaptable you have been in your approach and whether this has worked

- See adaptability in yourself as a sign of strength and not weakness

14   **BE RESPONSIVE**

BUILDING A REPERTOIRE of approaches will ensure that your coaching conversations are interesting with your taking pleasure in how you are widening your repertoire

The idea

The different approaches you bring might be based on encouraging someone to explore such aspects as:

* Who have you observed leading well in this situation and what did you learn?

* When have you been in a similar situation before and what did you learn about yourself and how best to handle this type of situation?

* When you dealt with this type of situation before and the outcome was not what you wanted, what was your learning and how it is applicable going forward?

* What emotional reactions does this type of situation elicit in you and how best do you handle them?

* Where do you want to get to in three months time and what needs to be in place for you to reach that position?

* What are the blockages that need to be overcome and how might you do that?

* What are three practical next steps which are attainable?

Having a sequence of questions which you draw from can enable you to help someone codify their experiences and provide a basis for developing a considered and realistic way forward.

Sometimes the best approach is to help someone start from current reality and move forward. For other people success comes from getting them to visualise a future state they want to reach and then work back from that position to clarify their next steps. The most appropriate approach will depend on someone's personal preferences and on the relative pressures in their current role.

Marilyn saw Jane as a practical person who needed to be clear about her own next steps. Talking about where she wanted to be in two years' time did not resonate with her, hence Marilyn focused on enabling Jane to think through her short-term objectives and to build relationships with new clients.

Marilyn recognised that the best way to start with Bill was to build agreement about where the business in his area might be in two years' time. The focus on the longer term would feed back into a revitalised intent to reach that destination. Marilyn smiled at herself as she recognised the way she was focusing on a different set of timescales in order to catch the imagination and motivation of these two very different individuals.

In practice

- Note down the type of approaches that you use in coaching others

- Keep extending that list in the light of experience

- Recognise that individuals have very different starting points about what will catch their imagination

- If one approach is not working be ready to switch your approach and say why you are doing so

- Celebrate when you use a different approach and it works

BE CLEAR ON THE TIME AVAILABLE

BRINGING CLARITY ABOUT the time available can help bring a focus to a conversation and ensure outcomes are as constructive as possible.

The idea

When I lead masterclasses and workshops I often ask people to work in pairs and invite them to coach each other on particular topics for five or six minutes. I might ask one of the pair to talk about an action they took that worked well and what they learnt from that experience, and invite the other person to be in coaching mode and to ask questions about how they are going to take that learning further forward and how they were going to apply that learning in similar, future situations.

I then switch the pair the other way so each individual has the experience of telling their story and being coached by their colleague, as well as doing the coaching of their colleague. The normal reaction in these situations is that it is possible to get much further than you might think in a short conversation and that being coached by someone in a focused way can be both enjoyable and productive.

One of the outcomes from the workshops is my encouragement to participants to be more open to coach each other in short conversations. The more the listening and coaching is two-way, with both people benefiting, the better.

Being clear at the start how long a conversation is going to be provides an important framework. If someone wants an urgent conversation it can be helpful to say they have your sole, undivided attention for 15 minutes but no longer. If the time available is one hour it may be possible to get into two subjects in reasonable depth. Knowing the pattern that works in conversations with a particular individual provides a discipline so that the time is used effectively. In an hour it is perhaps four or two topics that should be tackled.

Marilyn was clear that she needed to spend more time in conversation with Bill than Jane. She knew that working through a couple of issues and reaching a set of actions with Bill would take an hour, whereas with Jane 30 minutes would be fine. She agreed the timescales with the individuals. With both of them she got into a good rhythm and stuck to the time. Marilyn ensured that she always gave her sole, undivided attention which meant moving away from her desk and putting her iPhone away so she was not distracted.

In practice

- Be disciplined about bringing your sole, undivided attention

- Match the topics to be discussed to the time available

- Recognise the rhythms that work effectively with different people

- Be consistent, as far as possible, about the amount of time allowed

- Recognise that when dealing with a discrete topic you can get a long way in a short time

16 REACH AGREEMENT ON NEXT STEPS

To MAXIMISE THE benefits of a coaching conversation there needs to be agreement about the resulting approach an individual is going to take and their next steps.

The idea

A successful coaching conversation is rarely going to end in 12 precise action points. In a good conversation an individual will have been able to clarify their thinking and will have crystallized the broad approach they are going to take. There are likely to be some points of action but not too many.

Often coaching conversations that have the most profound effect lead to a change of attitude rather than precise next steps. If someone comes out of a conversation believing that they can make progress with new confidence then the knock-on effect can be significant.

Where a coaching conversation leads to a change in the level of self-belief or a clearer understanding of an issue, the impossible can become possible. Some people need the assurance of arriving at action points to feel that a coaching-type conversation has been worthwhile. Others are best left thinking overnight, mulling what they have been discussing and then reaching conclusions about next steps.

For many people it is helpful if a coaching conversation concludes with one of the participants writing down agreed next steps and action points. These can then provide a point of reference for a subsequent conversation as well as a discipline for the individual following upon the coaching conversation.

It is often useful to conclude a coaching conversation with an open-ended questions such as "what do you take away from this conversation?", or "what has this conversation helped crystallize about your approach and next steps?" It is always interesting to see what points have stuck in someone's memory.

Fiona felt she was having difficulty working with a particular government Minister. The Minister was always late for meetings and never looked interested in what she was saying. Fiona never looked forward to seeing the Minister but she knew she had to change her attitude. Fiona talked with Margaret who had been a private secretary to a previous Minister. Margaret encouraged Fiona to think about what she liked about the Minister and what conclusions she had been able to reach with the Minister.

Fiona recognised that there had been progress with the Minister even though she was annoyed by his personal behaviour which was more akin to that of a rude teenager than a responsible member of an elected Government. Fiona went out of the discussion with Margaret with a smile on her face: if she viewed the Minister as a sulky teenager she could handle his behaviour and focus on reaching conclusions with the Minister rather than be overwhelmed by her personal annoyance with him.

In practice

- Enable an individual to work out their next steps rather than telling them what to do

- See a change of attitude as a positive outcome

- Steer towards some agreed actions, without it being too long a list

- Agree on a suitable way of those conclusions being recorded

- Return in a subsequent conversation to review progress on agreed actions

17 CHOOSE THE FREQUENCY AND LOCATION OF CONVERSATIONS

Fundamental to the success of coaching conversations is choosing the right frequency and location for the conversations.

The idea

Coaching conversations that are too frequent can become a burden or a chore with limited progress between meetings. If the coaching conversations are too far apart their impact is lost and there is no continuity between the conversations. If someone is starting a new job or handling a very difficult situation there is merit in a reasonably frequent cycle, such as a sequence of three conversations with a month between meetings.

You want someone to look forward to a subsequent conversation and be ready with issues they want to discuss. My own preference is a cycle of meeting once every two months, although with some people a cycle of meeting once every three months or four months works fine. What matters is the rationale for a particular cycle and the mutual understanding about what is the right pattern.

The location of conversations is equally important. For some the best context is a quiet meeting room in an office. For others the most productive conversations are in a coffee bar, or a pub, or on a walk through a park, or on a train journey. What matters is audibility, not being disturbed, not being inhibited and not feeling under pressure to rush back into a work context. Both you and the individual need to be in an environment which is both relaxed and purposeful.

The same approach is essential for work with a team to be effective, with participants being present throughout and not disappearing in a stressed or self-important fashion to deal with a 'phone call.

Fiona knew that to get maximum benefit from her conversations with Margaret, she had to be calm and not feel annoyed by the Minister. If she was in an office environment there was a risk that annoyance with the Minister would bubble up in her mind. The place where she had the calmest conversations with Margaret was in a coffee bar 200 yards away from the office.

Margaret was astute enough to always suggest this particular location. With her hands wrapped around a warm cup of coffee Fiona felt more measured and more in control of her own emotions. When she finished the coffee she knew that she would have a plan for her next steps in coping with this Minister. Margaret and Fiona got into a pattern of having coffee for half-an-hour once every six weeks which helped keep Fiona's equilibrium in a reasonable place.

In practice

- Be deliberate in agreeing the frequency of conversations
- Choose a location that works well for each person
- Talk through the rhythm that is most productive
- Pitch the frequency slightly less often than is the preference of the individual so when the time comes they want the conversation
- Be clear about the length of time available
- Be sure to end on a positive note

18 ENSURE A REVIEW OF AN INDIVIDUAL'S PROGRESS

IF SOMEONE IS able to review their progress by drawing from external perspectives it will help them believe that they have taken constructive steps forward.

The idea

If an individual believes they have made progress that is probably the truth, but sometimes there can be self-delusion where an individual persuades themselves that they have made progress when this is not the case. On other occasions the individual may well have made good progress, but does not believe that they have made progress.

Asking somebody to summarize the progress that they observe in themselves can help them crystallize their progress. If they say that they are not making progress it can be helpful to ask what others might observe or what comments others might have made. Sometimes there is a risk that individuals will not acknowledge progress because they feel it will be a sign of complacency. This excessive humility can have a limiting effect on the progress someone is able to make.

A key contribution you can make is to observe the impact that an individual has and feedback with affirming comments. Sometimes it can be helpful to arrange some structured feedback which either you collect or through a 360° feedback tool. The most powerful feedback is often short examples of the positive consequences of someone's contribution and the outcomes it has led to. The good manager as coach will be nudging or steering people through using brief illustrations of good outcomes and lots of affirmation about what is going well.

When I work with groups I often invite them in pairs to talk about when they went out of their comfort zone in the last three weeks and surprised themselves by the progress made. Someone briefly telling their story can help someone reinforce the progress made.

When Margaret prepared to meet Fiona for a cup of coffee she would always collect a couple of stories about the contribution that Fiona had been able to make and the influence she had with the Minister. Margaret used these stories to help raise Fiona's self-confidence. Fiona trusted Margaret and recognised that Margaret would only use examples of what other people had said if they were true.

Margaret persuaded Fiona that she should ask the Minister for feedback. Fiona was pleasantly surprised by the comments from the Minister who volunteered that his behaviour was not always as helpful as it should be.

In practice

- Ask someone to review their own progress

- Bring your own observations about their progress

- Observe them in different contexts and collect stories about their contribution

- Use structured feedback approaches when you think that would be helpful

- Encourage someone to seek feedback from someone who they are unsure about and then to be ready to be surprised by what they hear

19 SEE EACH CONVERSATION AS PART OF A JOURNEY

ENABLING SOMEONE TO see a coaching conversation as an integral part of a journey and not just a one-off event can help reinforce the significance of such conversations.

The idea

Often the most productiove conversations can take place on a journey. When I was the Finance Director-General for David Blunkett as Secretary of State for Education and Employment I travelled next to him on a train journey to Sheffield early in his tenure which helped my understanding of his approach to finance.

Often the most productive conversations with teenagers are when you sit alongside them on a car journey. As you walk with a group of friends through the hills you can have enjoyable conversations with each person in turn as the combinations change after climbing over each stile.

As a manager in coaching mode we are on a journey with someone, sometimes ahead of them and sometimes alongside them. Often we want them to walk ahead on their own taking the initiative about the next steps on the route.

You want coaching conversations to be timely and encouraging. You might point out forthcoming rocks on the way or cliff edges to watch. You might refer to the impending panoramic view at the top of the hill. If you see each conversation as part of a journey you enable a conversation to move forward while recognising that the vista is changing all the time. You can invite them to look back and see the progress they have made, as well as look forward to their next steps and the opportunities ahead of them.

Whenever Fiona and Margaret met for coffee Margaret would invite Fiona to look back and see the progress she had made. Then Margaret invited Fiona to look forward at the steps she now wanted to take. Margaret shared stories from her own experience of working with different Ministers which helped Fiona see Margaret as an experienced companion on this journey.

Margaret was able to help Fiona see her journey in a wider context so it was not all about the relationship with this particular Minister, but was about the wider contribution she was able to make in the department and the learning that she was taking forward.

In practice

- Reflect on whether using the language of journey is helpful or unhelpful

- Consciously enable someone to look back and see the progress they have made

- See your role as pointing out what might not be immediately visible in terms of risks and future encouragements

- Be conscious when you walk alongside someone, when you might be leading them, and when you want them to walk ahead

- Recognise that the pace of the journey will vary and be conscious when you are deliberately slowing it down or speeding it up

20 USE SHORT, FOCUSED CONVERSATIONS WELL

SHORT, FOCUSED CONVERSATIONS can be just as significant as long ones when the purpose of the conversation is clear and a next step is crystallized.

The idea

When I work with large groups and ask them to coach each other in pairs the topic might be something like, 'tell a story about something you did that went wrong and what did you learn from that experience'. I then invite the other person in the pair to ask why that learning was significant and what the individual is now going to do to embed that learning. The feedback is always, "I did not realise how far you can get in five minutes when you are focused on one question".

I then invite people to use the five-minute approach more often. I suggest that the approach works best when it is mutual and when both people can talk through a story and get the benefit of responding to some thoughtful questions from a colleague.

The key to success is about the quality of interaction and being able to give someone complete attention. If you feel that someone is absorbed in what you are saying you are much more likely to be open in what you say. When someone asks you two good questions that help you clarify your progress and crystallize your next steps, a brief conversation can have a profound effect on your own self-confidence and next steps.

The normal pattern of coaching conversations will be a reflective conversation over say, an hour or an hour and a half, but a valuable part of the repertoire is short, focused conversations on a particular issue. Having a limited timeframe can often enable someone to get to the nub of a point and for you to focus on only one or two questions.

Where you have a sequence of coaching conversations with an individual it can be helpful to say that you will be available between meetings for short, single topic conversations where the individual and you both bring a discipline about shaping the issue with the conversation getting to the nub of the issue and ending up with clarity about a next step.

Fiona knew that if she had a concern about how to work with the Minister on a specific issue, she could ask Margaret for five minutes of her time. They developed a discipline whereby Fiona would briefly summarize the issue and her proposed way of handling it with Margaret bringing a brief perspective or asking a couple of questions, and then Fiona briefly reviewing what she was going to do in the light of that reaction or question. These discussions were short and not prolonged. Margaret was happy to help in this way provided the conversations were a maximum of 10 minutes.

In practice

- Include short, focused conversations in your repertoire

- Bring sole, undivided attention and recognise your role is to bring one reflection or one or two questions

- Ensure the objective is limited and clear

- Build an understanding that short means short

- Encourage short, two-way coaching conversations among team members as part of their way of working with each other

COACHING CONVERSATIONS

BALANCE THE LONGER TERM AND THE SHORTER TERM

INTERLINKING SHORT-TERM AND long-term learning ensures a more considered future alongside effective, short-term learning.

The idea

An individual may have a problem they are dealing with in the short-term that is all consuming. The way they handle a short-term problem reinforces patterns of thought and emotional reactions which will be part of their approach over the longer term. After an individual has worked through a short-term issue, it is always worth asking what they have learnt from this experience and what will be the relevance of that learning in future, similar situations.

The danger can be that someone rushes onto the next issue they need to tackle without reflecting on their learning from handling the immediate issue. The learning can be just as profound if the outcome was success or failure in the short-term.

Enabling someone to think through how they would handle parallel issues in the future is both about how they prepare and about their attitude of mind. Once a manager has handled a difficult member of staff successfully, they will have learnt a set of approaches that work. The likelihood is that their confidence will be stronger when handling a similar type of situation in the future.

Balancing the longer term and the shorter term is about enabling someone to be clear what experiences they need in the short-term to equip them to do what they would like to do in the longer term.

Defining a competence that an individual wants to have in the future and then working with them on how they will develop that competence in the short-term can provide a very good catalyst for progress.

Rashida recognised that if she was promoted she would need to be able to speak confidently in front of large groups of people. She was currently apprehensive about doing so. Her boss, Vic, encouraged her to do presentations to small groups of staff. Rashida helped lead a young people's organisation and Vic encouraged her to do presentations for this organisation. Vic observed Rashida doing some presentations at work and encouraged her to reflect on what had gone well and less well. He gave her some practical pointers but allowed Rashida to develop her confidence in giving presentations. The long-term goal of being promoted had given her the incentive to practice giving presentations in the short-term which, surprisingly, she began to enjoy doing.

In practice

- See each short-term challenge as a way of encouraging an individual's longer term development

- Always seek to draw out the learning from the way an individual has dealt with shorter term issues

- See the learning as both about practicalities and attitudes of mind

- Start from longer term aspirations to identify shorter term development needs

- Ensure you enable someone to ask good questions about the link between the long-term and the short-term

RECOGNISE HOW INDIVIDUALS LEARN

EACH INDIVIDUAL LEARNS in a different way and at a different rate. When we recognise how individuals learn we can adjust our approach to match their needs.

The idea

Some people need to know all the theory first before they are willing to begin to experiment. They have had to have read the instruction book in full before they are ready to start the new appliance. For others learning is more experiential: the instruction book is read after they have experimented with pressing various knobs and buttons.

Some people learn by observing and reflecting and then taking forward steps gradually. Others learn by starting to talk and crystallizing their understanding as words flow out of their mouth.

In coaching conversations some learn best by being prompted with questions that make them reflect on their experience. They need silence to process their thoughts. The time between coaching conversations will be particularly important as the ideas that come up in a coaching conversation will need to germinate before they blossom into something fresh and different.

For others the crystallization of the thinking comes within the coaching conversation as they talk through issues and begin to shape their own next steps. For these individuals there can be 'light going on' moments in a coaching conversation when something falls into place, or there is a clarity about the way forward

It is very important for some individuals to leave a coaching conversation with two or three practical actions they are going to take. For others the best takeaway is a mantra which they can hold in their mind such as 'I am going to be more assertive about X ', or 'I am going to make a decision by Y'. For others at the end of the session they might note the key factors that they need to weigh up before making a decision and they know how they are going to weight those factors.

Vic knew that Rashida took time to come to decisions. He saw his role as sowing seeds and then letting Rashida reflect. Pressing her to come to a precise conclusion at the end of a coaching conversation could make her defensive. Vic knew that Rashida needed time after a coaching conversation to process her thoughts.

The pattern that worked well was for Vic to say at the end of a coaching conversation that he would be interested to know what Rashida had concluded after a few days. She would then send him a short note, summarizing in a couple of sentences, her conclusion. Vic was pleased he had found a pattern that worked well with Rashida.

In practice

* Observe how individuals learn

* Go with the grain of the way an individual learns

* Pace the conversation in a way which maximizes the individual's learning

* Ensure the way you end a coaching conversation is consistent with the way the individual is likely to crystallize and take forward their learning from that conversation

* Always remember that other people learn differently from the way you learn

23 ENABLE SOMEONE TO LIVE THEIR VALUES

IF SOMEONE IS living their values they will be more fulfilled, more engaged and more effective.

The idea

The underlying coaching approach which I use was set out in my book, *The Four Vs of Leadership: Vision, Values, Value-added and Vitality*. These four Vs embrace: what is your vision of the leader you want to be, what is the value-added you bring now as a leader and want to bring in the future, and what are your sources of vitality and how do you nurture them? But central to this approach is the importance of the individual knowing their values and knowing what living those values to the full means for them.

If you know what values are most important to an individual it gives you a valuable insight into the way they think and act. The values that come from our cultural and family backgrounds shape the way we think and respond. The values we have embraced through our life become a crucial part of the way we make decisions. Building an understanding of someone so you appreciate their values and where they come from can provide a framework to enable you to ask good questions and help them steer their own thinking.

The question, "what are your values telling you is the right thing to do in this situation?" can help flag up key considerations. Often an individual will balance two values which appear conflicting. If an individual is not performing well the manager might want to be compassionate to the individual, but also caring about other members of staff who are detrimentally affected by this individual's limited performance. Enabling someone to address how the value of fairness applies to both the individual and the wider group can enable them develop the resolve to tackle this type of dilemma.

Rashida thought that the approach taken by one of her staff bordered on bullying but was hesitant to tackle this person as she was effective in lots of ways. Vic encouraged Rashida to think through what was the right thing to do in addressing this behaviour rather than just the expedient thing to do. Rashida knew that this behaviour had to be tackled even if it led to a short-term dip in the individual's performance.

In practice

- Encourage an individual to talk about the values that are most important to them and where they come from

- Explore the link between someone's vision for their own future and the values that underpin that vision

- Enable someone to explore situations where their values might be in conflict

- Enable individuals or teams to reflect openly on their values and when they are in danger of being overridden

- Share your own experiences of when your values have been challenged and how you addressed this

24 ENSURE HARSH REALITY IS FACED UP TO

HARSH REALITY CANNOT be ignored. It has to be faced up to and addressed.

The idea

A good question for the manager to hold in their mind is, "in what way is this individual blinkered?" We are all blinkered in some ways. Shielding our eyes is important in order to focus our attention and to blank out thoughts or beliefs that are going to get in the way.

When an individual is working on a project there will always be the fear that the project might not succeed. Such a fear can be all consuming and mean that an individual's creativity and energy is sapped, hence the importance of encouraging someone to box those fears so they do not contaminate their creativity and energy in dealing with current, high priority considerations.

On the other hand an individual who ignores harsh reality is short-sighted. If an individual is about to run into a brick wall, the sooner they see the brick wall the better. Part of an effective coaching conversation is about enabling someone to recognise objectively and calmly the harsh reality in front of them, and then enabling the individual to work through potential consequences.

Asking questions such as, "what is the harsh reality that is unavoidable in this situation?" can be helpful in focusing the mind. But linked with this question needs to be an encouraging way of thinking about the future with questions like, "what opportunities might this situation open up?" or "how might you be better equipped to handle this harsh reality than others?"

Enabling someone to reflect on how they have learnt from harsh reality in the past will remind them of the inner resolve that is within them and how constructive outcomes have flowed from the most unpromising of situations.

A recent customer survey suggested that Rashida's team was viewed less positively by customers than previously. Rashida was tempted to brush aside these results as the team had been very busy. Vic asked Rashida what was the harsh reality here that she needed to address. This question helped to focus Rashida's thinking: she accepted that there were problems that needed to be addressed. When Vic pressed her on what were the opportunities going forward Rashida developed a forward plan which involved her spending more focused time with her staff and working through how they were going to respond more effectively to some groups of customers.

In practice

- Face people up to harsh reality in a considered rather than brutal way

- Link together reality and opportunity

- Allow someone the time to recognise and remove their own blinkers

- Share something of your own experience of handling harsh reality

- Enable someone to recognise how they have handled harsh reality well in the past

SEEK FEEDBACK ON WHAT HAS WORKED

COACHING CONVERSATIONS SHOULD be dynamic with you learning as much as the individual you are working with.

The idea

Where coaching conversations are productive, both participants are learning. The coachee builds a new perspective and clarifies their approach going forward. The manager as coach learns more about the situation, the individual they are working with and themselves.

If you are to enjoy the coaching element of your work as a manager you need to keep developing your skills of listening, questioning, engaging and steering. As you do more coaching-type conversations you will find yourself varying your pace and using a wider range of questions. You will enable others to look at issues from different angles. Individuals will be more willing to talk about their emotional reactions to a situation, rather than be dominated by their emotional reactions. You should see a greater lightness in others, and in yourself.

Seeking feedback from the people you have been working with about what has worked well or less well is central to your further development. Asking someone, 'what has landed for you in our conversation?' will give you good feedback about what has been remembered from the conversation. There may be messages here about the relative effectiveness of different parts of the conversation if some elements of a conversation appear to have been forgotten.

Asking the direct question, "what elements of my approach work well and what work less well?" is important. What is said in response will be a valuable prompt. Remember that feedback says as much about the individual giving feedback as it does about you; hence treat feedback with care and use it to identify overall patterns.

Vic asked Rashida whether his approach had been helpful. Rashida was grateful for the space Vic gave her to reflect between conversations. Rashida said that often what was most valuable was one reflection or story, or a question that Vic posed which Rashida then reflected on between the conversations. Rashida commented that it was counter-productive if Vic tried to push her to reach a conclusion too quickly, but it worked well if Rashida sent an e-mail a few days later saying which had crystallized about what she was going to do next.

In practice

- Observe carefully what has been remembered from different parts of a coaching conversation

- Seek feedback on what elements of your approach work well or less well

- Keep evolving your approach and widening it in the light of the feedback you receive

- Look for patterns in the feedback

- See coaching conversations as a continuous type of learning for you and the people you are working with.

26 REVIEW THE OUTCOMES AFTER A PERIOD

REGULAR REVIEWS OF outcomes will provide a good guide as to when conversations should stop, continue or change direction.

The idea

Endings come more easily to some people than others. Some people enjoy concluding a relationship, drawing a line under it and moving on. For others ending a sequence of coaching conversations can be painful and unnerving. Someone might feel that if they stop talking an issue through with somebody they will inevitably go backwards in their approach.

Sometimes it must be right to say we have made as much progress as we are going to make in this conversation or in this sequence of conversations. The individual has constructed a way forward and it is now time for them to go forward alone without the independent reassurance that comes from a coaching conversation. When the cyclist is climbing a mountain they do it without the cycling coach at their shoulder, even though the words of the cycling coach may be ringing in their ears.

Often it is right after a number of coaching-type conversations to be clear on the outcomes so far and to say, "you are on your own". The coaching conversations might continue at a later date, or they might move to another subject. I have worked with a number of people over six or seven years, but we are regularly re-contracting. We move on from working towards one set of outcomes to another set of outcomes and are varying the frequency and pace of our conversations to meet new requirements.

There can be good outcomes from short coaching conversations. Short, focused conversations on individual subjects can lead to a new insight or clarity about a particular action which can enable someone to change direction. A good outcome might be one, simple point.

When Gemma started her new role as team leader, Hazel, her boss, worked with her over three sessions about stepping up into leadership. Gemma developed an inner belief that she could do the job well and some key principles about how she would handle the early months. Hazel was positive about Gemma's early progress. They agreed to do a review in three months' time with Hazel standing back more and letting Gemma build on what she had learned over the first three months.

In practice

- Set a time-frame when a review of progress would be appropriate

- Agree what type of review is right

- Recognise that the use of short conversations with one outcome can be very powerful

- Leave enough space between conversations so that an individual has to take forward their own action

- Review carefully what might be going wrong if there are no outcomes

BE MINDFUL OF THE INDIVUDAL'S ENERGY LEVELS

SOMEONE'S ENERGY LEVELS are a very good indicator of their level of engagement and motivation.

The idea

Observing someone's energy levels can provide a very good indicator of what is going on in their mind and in their emotions. Energy levels are affected by the rhythm of a day. There can be exhaustion following a difficult meeting or an emotional lift after a meeting has gone well.

What matters is identifying what is the underlying energy level and whether that energy level is easily knocked. Is the energy focused or is it seeping away and being drained through difficult and emotionally jarring exchanges?

Open-ended questions like, "what is lifting your energy at the moment?" or "what is sapping your energy at the moment?" can provide a very good starting point to enable someone to talk through what is going well, and what is causing them angst. Enabling someone to work through what aspects of a role gives them energy and what dilutes their energy can help indicate whether they feel more or less confident in their approach.

When Gemma began her new role Hazel was conscious that Gemma talked energetically about most of the responsibilities but began to talk more slowly and diffidently when referring to the finance lead. Hazel asked Gemma why her tone of voice and energy level was different when she referred to the finance lead. Gemma talked about her uncertainties in dealing with some of the financial issues.

Hazel talked with Gemma about how she might build a stronger relationship with the finance lead and develop her own understanding of some of the financial considerations. Over time Gemma began to feel a bit more confident and recognised that her energy and commitment in building the right understanding and relationships on finance were getting a bit better. Hazel was glad that she had used her reading of Gemma's energy levels as an indicator of a problem which needed further exploration.

In practice

- Observe the energy levels in those you are working as an indicator of their engagement and motivation

- Discount the effect of the ups and downs of the day in order to see what are the underlying energy levels

- Encourage someone to reflect on what gives them energy inside and outside the office and how they can do the activities which help them grow their energy

- Recognise in someone's tone of voice what the commitment of energy is to reaching a particular outcome

- Recognise that everyone's energy level needs to be recharged. You have an important role encouraging them to spend enough time recharging their energy

28 USE YOURSELF AS A BAROMETER

Observing your own reactions and the emotions of people and situations gives you valuable data about what is going on beneath the surface.

The idea

We use ourselves as a barometer all the time. When we enter a room we immediately gauge the temperature: we slightly shiver because it is cold, or we take a sweater off if it is hot. In any conversation we are experiencing emotional reactions all the time which are providing us with valuable data. These emotional reactions need testing as they may be wrong, but they are valuable data nonetheless. When you enter a room that feels cold you may want to check with others how they are feeling about the temperature rather than immediately turning up the dial on the heater.

When you are in a coaching conversation with someone it is valuable to use yourself as a barometer. What am I thinking and feeling about what the individual is saying? Do I bring a wider perspective from other parallel situations or because I have observed this person in previous contexts? What are the intuitive senses I have about what is going on in the situation they are describing? Such an intuitive sense will come from a range of different antennae.

Good coaching as a manager or leader flows from letting that intuitive sense feed into the questions or approach you use. If you have a strong emotional reaction it can be worth sharing that reaction as an observation which can lead to discussion about what is your reaction saying about the situation. If your reaction is, 'all is not lost' it is probably worth saying. If a particular picture or image comes to mind it can be worth sharing that picture or image and discussing what might be the parallels. If you can see an analogy or a metaphor that might work it can be worth talking it through.

When Gemma and Hazel were talking about the way Gemma was tackling her new role, Hazel observed her own emotional reactions. Hazel was conscious when she warmed to what Gemma was doing, and when Gemma's approach left her feeling cold. Hazel was careful not to use this reaction to prejudge whether Gemma was doing the right thing or not, but Hazel knew it gave her valuable data if she listened to her own emotions. At times she would say, "I have warmed to your approach". Once or twice Hazel said a particular approach, "left her feeling a bit cold" but she wasn't sure why. This type of comment produced good reflective conversation, with Gemma thinking again whether she was using an appropriate approach or not.

In practice

- Observe your own emotional reactions to see what data they are giving you

- See yourself as a barometer recognising when you warm to something and when it leaves you feeling cold

- Be ready to share how you feel about a particular course of action if you think that would be helpful

- Put forward reactions as thoughts for the individual to consider and not instructions for them to follow

- Check whether your barometer readings tie in with those of others

ALLOW SOMEONE TO FIND THEIR OWN WAY TO SOLVE A PROBLEM

COACHING CONVERSATIONS ARE about enabling and equipping someone to solve a problem and are not about solving the problem for them.

The idea

We are all conscious of the temptation to say to someone, "If I were you I would do it this way". Most of us have a desire to tell someone what to do based on our own experience. This can be the right approach when it is a technical question. When I am wrestling with a piece of modern technology what I need are some precise, clear instructions, preferably written down simply, which enable me to reach the outcomes I need quickly and with a minimum amount of wasted energy or time.

On other occasions a precise set of instructions will produce a non-compliant reaction. I do not want to be told that the best place to go on holiday in August is Italy. But I am very happy to explore in a conversation the pros and cons of different destinations to equip me to reach my own conclusion.

When you have a coaching conversation with someone there are moments when it is right to be setting out some guidelines and times when it is right to counsel against an approach. It can be helpful to set out from your own experience five or six key principles about how to chair meetings well. But it is for the individual to sift through that guidance and to reflect on what is going to work best for them to enable them to chair meetings in the most constructive way. The individual needs to decide on their own approach to chairing meetings well, but setting out your own experience and what you observe in others can provide useful input.

Inviting someone to reflect on how they have found a solution to similar problems before can help them draw on their previous experience. It can be helpful for them to reflect on how they have handled similar problems outside work and what approaches they have used. This sometimes leads to 'light going on moments' when they recognise that an approach they have used in persuading their children to do something could also be applied to a difficult colleague.

Hazel was full of ideas about how Gemma could start her role successfully, but Hazel rationed herself to suggesting a couple of pointers in each conversation. Hazel knew that if she made too many suggestions, Gemma would feel overwhelmed. What mattered was Hazel giving Gemma space to devise her own solutions with a few prompts which were particularly about relative priorities.

In practice

- Hold back when you want to solve someone's problems for them

- Ask how they have solved similar problems at work in the past

- Invite them to reflect on how they have solved similar problems outside work

- Ration yourself about the number of practical steers you are going to give

- Differentiate between giving one or two practical tips, and talking through wider considerations that might be borne in mind

30 BRING RESPECT FOR THE INDIVIDUAL'S EXPERIENCE AND QUALITIES

RECOGNISING AN INDIVIDUAL's experience and qualities reinforces their belief in their own capabilities.

The idea

I can recall, as a member of the Combined Cadet Force at school, being drilled to march in formation. The Sergeant Major would yell at us as if we were idiots and chastise us whenever we got something wrong. The result was an intense dislike of the Sergeant Major; it felt like a public mauling to be told that we were abysmal at marching in step. Being yelled at did not raise our motivation or commitment one jot.

A valuable question to hold in your mind is how do you show respect for the individual's experience and qualities so that they want to build on those qualities and become increasingly effective. The good leader as coach is the exact opposite to the drill sergeant who is determined to shout troops into submission. You are trying to increase an individual's belief in themselves and to enable them to be curious about what they can now achieve. Your role is to catch their imagination about what is possible and how they might move on to bring out the best in themselves and others.

Your role is to combine positive affirmation with encouraging a sense of exploration and stretch. Through demonstrating respect for each part of someone's previous experience you are boosting their self-esteem and their self-awareness, particularly as you demonstrate respect their learning from what has gone wrong in the past. Playing back to individuals the positive qualities you see in them and others have identified in them is never wasted.

Hazel recognised that Gemma's confidence would go up and down as she started this new role. Helen was conscious that she needed to keep telling Gemma about the qualities she observed in her. Gemma needed to keep hearing those qualities and to know that she had the respect of her boss at a time when the learning process was tough in this new role. Hazel recognised that the repetition of these qualities was a necessary part of keeping Gemma's confidence high and building up those qualities as she stepped up in responsibility.

In practice

- Be clear in your own mind about what you particular respect about an individual's experience and qualities

- Articulate that respect regularly, recognising when the individual needs that reassurance

- Observe what type of comments from you reinforce the right type of confidence and approach

- As someone develops in their role, articulate what you have observed in those developing qualities

- Observe what is the link between what you say and an individual's motivation

- Vary the words and use different examples so that the individual believes what you say because it is up to date

ENSURE PITFALLS AND RISKS ARE UNDERSTOOD

WHEN PITFALLS AND risks are understood there can be realism about next steps and how they are taken further forward.

The idea

When someone approaches you with enthusiasm and intent to do a job well, the last thing you want to do is dampen their enthusiasm. You do not want to describe the pitfalls and risks in such a way that their energy dissipates and they have no desire to tackle these risks.

The outcome you want is that an individual is aware of the pitfalls and key risks, and knows how they are going to handle them in a way which is realistic and measured. Handling a risk or pitfall is a crucial part of the way an individual wants to learn.

The new teacher in the classroom comes with a sense of vocation and energy. They understand the pitfalls about lack of discipline in the classroom and hopefully come equipped with some practical approaches. The leader as coach will be raising questions about what are the pitfalls and how to address them.

The leader as coach is likely to focus on the key risks so that an individual is able to focus on one risk at a time. Deluging someone with comments about all the risks they face is not likely to enable them to develop the resolve and the plan to handle each risk in turn. Your job is to bring honesty about pitfalls and risks without overwhelming someone. They need to go out of conversations with you believing that the pitfalls and risks are manageable even if they might be difficult to handle.

Norma was excited about the additional responsibilities she had been given at an investment bank. Her boss, Hassan, was pleased to have her in his team. Hassan appreciated Norma's positive attitude and her ability to build personal relationships quickly. Hassan wanted to ensure that Norma understood the new sector she was working in and recognised some of the pitfalls and risks.

Hassan was concerned that some of the client organisations might try and take advantage of Norma's newness to the area and get her to agree to deals too early. Hassan talked through with Norma the characteristics of the different client organisations and what approach they were likely to take. Hassan drew attention to the risks and suggested some approaches, but he knew Norma had to learn from experience who she could trust and who she needed to be wary of. Hassan had periodic, short conversations with Norma over the first couple of weeks to see how she was progressing and flagged up gradually some of the on-going risks, ensuring that Norma understood their implications.

In practice

- Be clear in your own mind what are the pitfalls and risks

- Talk through the pitfalls and risks one at a time

- Present pitfalls and risks as manageable and not overwhelming

- Equip someone to reach their own view on how they handle pitfalls and risks

- Review periodically and briefly how pitfalls and risks are being viewed by an individual and by teams

BELIEVE THAT GOOD CAN COME OUT OF ANY SITUATION

BE RELENTLESS IN believing that good can come out of any situation however difficult or unpleasant that situation has been.

The idea

One of the most important contributions that a leader as coach can make is to bring a mindset that however difficult a situation is there can always be constructive outcomes. Believing that good can come out of any situation leads to an attitude of mind which looks for positive outcomes, whatever the pain or aggravation of the current experience.

As someone explains a difficult situation they are handling, inviting them to reflect on, "what positive outcome could there be at the end of this process?" helps create a positive attitude of mind and enables them to be less daunted.

Sharing examples of situations you were involved in that appeared to be a failure but which turned out to have positive consequences can be helpful. Talking about the experience of an abysmal presentation which led to looking at a project plan from first principles again can be an encouragement.

Talking through an example of losing confidence in a situation and how you then rebuilt your confidence to deal with similar, future situations can provide a helpful story for someone facing a similar situation. I am conscious that I draw in my coaching work far more on my failures than successes as a means of enabling others to learn.

Norma had two or three disagreements with a couple of her colleagues. A difference about a technical approach had turned into a heated and emotional argument. Norma regretted the emotions she had shown and feared that the relationships were irredeemable.

Hassan encouraged her to think about what good could come out of this situation. Norma said that she would now treat these colleagues with more respect and listen to and engage with them more thoughtfully and carefully. In a slightly less busy period Norma suggested that she and the two colleagues had coffee together. They found some points of common interest and gradually built up greater openness in their relationship. Two or three months later they were able to laugh at how they had 'blown up' at each other. Their working relationship was now stronger because of the way they had coped with the disagreement. It had now moved into another and more positive phase.

In practice

- Encourage someone to believe that there can be good outcomes from any situation
- Enable someone to be clear how they want to redeem a difficult situation
- Encourage someone to take one step at a time in building a constructive, working relationship going forward
- Enable someone to recognise that it can take time to reach constructive outcomes
- Be patient when others are not yet ready to be constructive

WALK ALONGSIDE SOMEONE AT A MEASURED DISTANCE

As YOU WALK alongside someone at a measured distance you are a source of encouragement and can provide prompts, but it is their journey and not yours.

The idea

When a toddler starts to walk, the parent walks alongside and may guide the toddler or help them get up when they fall. But the parent knows that the toddler needs to walk on their own if they are to become confident in their ability to walk. The toddler wants the reassurance of the parent nearby but wants to experiment and see if they can walk successfully from one side of the room to another.

The 'well done' from the parent encourages the toddler to walk across the room again. The toddler is glad that the parent is in the vicinity but is determined to walk on their own and begins to delight in their new-found freedom.

The image of walking alongside someone at a measured distance can sum up the role of a manager with a new member of staff or with someone who is taking on new responsibilities. The manager must not get in the way or precipitate a reaction whereby the staff member wants to give the problem back to the manager. Keeping your distance is crucial while still providing the reassurance that you are understanding and aware of what is happening.

Norma was not finding it straightforward to build the right relationship with some client organisations. Hassan gave her some practical ideas but wanted to keep his distance. Success for Hassan was ensuring that the clients talked to Norma and not him hence what mattered was enabling Norma to build the right sort of long-term relationship with the clients with Hassan only being involved at key review meetings.

On a couple of occasions Hassan had to say firmly to the client that they were to work with Norma on a day-to-day basis, and should not approach him other than at the six-monthly review meetings. Hassan knew he was taking a calculated risk through applying this approach in order to enable Norma to grow fully into her responsibilities and establish the right relationship with the client organisations.

In practice

- Keep your distance when you are tempted to get too involved

- Allow someone to learn to walk and run in their own strength

- Be a source of encouragement without impeding someone's learning

- Be visible only to those people you want to be visible to

- Be ready to step well aside when your job is done

34 ALLOW FOR SILENCE AND QUIETNESS

PROGRESS CAN COME from silence and quietness as well as through activity and words.

The idea

When Clive Woodward was rebuilding the England Rugby Union team in 1999/2000 he introduced a different approach to second-half thinking. The half-time routine involved two minutes of absolute silence when the players thought about the performance, towelled down and put on new kit.

Following three minutes of the coaches' assessment, and three minutes final word from the coach and the captain, there was a further two minutes silence visualising the kick-off. Clive Woodward used the symbolic act of putting on clean shirts combined with the use of silence to create a renewed mindset for the second half.

We live in a fast world where words imply action. We can listen to the words of anyone any time using information technology. But often the most powerful moments are times of silence when we reflect and resolve what we are going to do next. Often the best moments of preparation are silent moments when we identify two or three key points we want to make in a particular meeting.

The coach as leader allows for silence and quietness in the conversation. Sometimes an individual goes quiet and needs to process an emotional reaction. On other occasions the manager as coach can suggest that an individual takes a couple of minutes to reflect on their next steps in the way they handle a situation. A good technique can be to suggest a three minute break to get a cup of coffee which allows someone to think through their next steps.

Norma and Hassan were crowded into a massive room which contained a large number of desks. There was a constant buzz of activity with an underlying sound of people's voices on the telephones. Hassan knew that if Norma was to change her approach to situations or individuals she needed to reflect more.

Hassan would often go for a conversation with Norma in a quiet space or sometimes out to a coffee bar. He knew that he had to create a sense of quietness for Norma to recalibrate her thinking. Hassan was comfortable in conversation with Norma when there were periods of silence: he knew that these moments could often be the most productive parts of the conversation.

In practice

- See silence as productive

- Recognise when quietness is essential for someone to think through next steps

- Allow silence to happen and do not feel that you have to fill the space

- Build a mutual understanding about how silence can be used productively

- Recognise how long a period of quietness an individual might need to be clear about their own next steps

ENABLE AN INDIVIDUAL TO DRAW FROM THEIR OWN EXPERIENCE

WE ALL BRING much wider levels of experience to work situations than we recognise.

The idea

The question, "what type of activity, which may be relevant to your work, have you been involved in this weekend?" can produce a quizzical look. The enquiry might be interpreted as, "how much work have you done this weekend?" What an individual does in their time outside work is often much more transferable into the work situation than they readily appreciate.

The individual who is in a leadership role in a voluntary organisation such as a sports club, a community organisation, a faith-based charity or a church will have developed a wealth of experience of working with volunteers and seeking to reach agreement with a disparate group of individuals.

The parent is continually negotiating with their children seeking to balance different priorities. The parent who says at work that they are no good at negotiating may not be recognising the transferable skills they bring from their role as a parent.

There is a risk that we all focus on the applicability of our recent work experience, when the reality is that we can draw on experience from a range of different roles. When I am preparing someone for an interview I encourage them to think through what is the mix of experience they have had in the last 15 years which is relevant to the expectations of the potential employer.

Hassan knew that Norma had worked in central government prior to joining the investment banking firm. Hassan encouraged Norma to reflect on the skills she had learnt about handling the politics in government which she could transfer into her new role.

Hassan also knew that Norma was vice-captain of a hockey team. Hassan encouraged Norma to think through what she had learnt as the member of a leadership team of the hockey club that she could transfer into her approach at the investment bank. The parallels were much stronger than Norma had imagined in terms of recognising people's strengths and ensuring robust resilience under attack.

In practice

- Share examples of where your wider experience has enabled you to be a more effective leader

- Encourage an individual to reflect on the approaches they are using outside work and how they might be applied inside work

- Encourage them to see previous experience as relevant and not irrelevant

- Stimulate individuals to share stories about how their wider activities inform their approach to work

- Enable people to talk about instances when they have transferred approaches they have used with their children and young people into a work context

36 CELEBRATE PROGRESS

We all respond to positive affirmation, hence the importance of always celebrating progress.

The idea

I often include in a coaching conversation a passage about, "the progress I observe in you is..." We often think it is trite to say to someone the progress we observe in them. Our mindset might be that such comments border on flattery and could appear disingenuous.

The truth is that we all benefit from and like affirmation. As a toddler and then as a youngster at school it was positive affirmation that enabled us to be confident in walking, speaking and interacting with others. We all benefit from 'being cheered from the sidelines' and yet we are often very coy about giving and receiving praise in the workplace.

Vague phrases like 'thank you' or 'good progress' are fine up, to a point, but if they are not specific they are not received as carrying much significance. The more specific we are about identifying and acknowledging progress the more credible those comments will be. The more specific the comment the more likely it is to encourage repeat behaviour.

Starting a coaching conversation by asking, "what progress are you celebrating?" can help put someone into a positive frame of mind reflecting on good points rather than going straightaway into what they are finding difficult. Starting from the progress in the most complicated issue can create a positive perspective that it is going to be possible to move into a productive next phase.

William was the incumbent Minister at an inner city church: his Curate, Rachel, was not finding the transition to her new role easy. Rachel was used to working in a world where people did what they said they were going to do. Rachel found it difficult to work with volunteers who did not always take forward what they had agreed to do.

William encouraged Rachel to think of examples where the volunteers had taken forward action well and what aspects of her approach had enabled these individuals to be motivated. William was conscious that Rachel needed to believe that she had made progress in order to be confident enough to talk to and encourage others to take more of a lead in working with children and young people.

In practice

- Recognise the effect of positive affirmation on you

- Note down what individuals have done well to draw on in future conversations

- Articulate examples of progress in a way which is specific and recognises the contribution of the individual

- Repeat examples of progress on a periodic basis

- When you share an example of progress look as if you mean it, and say it with a smile on your face

ENABLE INDIVIDUALS TO CRYSTALLIZE THEIR LEARNING

FINDING THE WAY in which an individual crystallizes their learning can help ensure that the learning is embedded for the future.

The idea

An important question to ask someone when you bring a coaching approach is, "how do you crystallize your learning?" For some people talking through what they have been learning is the way it becomes embedded. Talking with a trusted colleague or friend about how they have handled an issue is crucial to crystallizing their learning.

For other people the best approach is to use a notebook to write down at the end of each week what they have learnt during the course of the week. The value of this approach is that it enables someone to look back at their learning over a number of weeks.

The coach as manager can play a crucial role in enabling someone to be clear what is the process that needs to be in place so the individual can crystallize their learning and remind them of the journey of learning they have been on.

A supplementary question can be, "how are you going to reinforce that learning over the next few weeks?" If someone has chaired a meeting successfully they need to chair more meetings in order to further embed that learning. If someone has given a presentation to 100 people and learnt techniques that work well for them, doing another presentation a few weeks later will further embed a successful approach.

Rachel was apprehensive about speaking to the very eclectic congregation at the church which varied widely in age, education and social background. Her early talks were too theoretical. With William's help Rachel introduced more stories into her talks which became more practical.

Rachel began to see how she could interlink stories and practical approaches more readily with the biblical passage of the day. William encouraged her to continue to use an approach that had begun to work for her which thereby became more embedded. Rachel gradually felt more confident when she was speaking in front of this very diverse group of people.

In practice

- Ask about what someone is learning

- Encourage them to find an approach which works for them in terms of recording their learning

- Encourage them to reflect on how they are going to embed this learning

- Suggest that individuals periodically reflect on what they have learnt over recent months and enjoy the progress they have made in their learning

ENCOURAGE CONTRIBUTIONS WITHIN WIDER TEAMS

LEARNING COMES FROM making your own contribution, and from your experience and contribution within a wider team.

The idea

The mindset for many individuals is that their success depends on what they do as an individual. But success is often dependent on their contribution to a wider team. The success of a footballer is not just dependent on the goals they score. The good footballer passes the ball to their team members in an efficient and timely way. The good footballer covers for other people and enables them to move into a space where a team member can pass the ball to them. The outstanding football team will be known for its teamwork rather than individual virtuoso performances.

The leader as coach can play a valuable role in enabling an individual to look more widely than at their own specific responsibilities. The question, "how do you want to contribute to the wider team?" cannot be ignored. The individual will rarely respond by saying, "I do not wish to contribute to the wider team". As team leader you may want to suggest particular areas where an individual can contribute, but you may want to leave the final decision to the individual to ensure they are committed to a positive outcome. Sharing examples of where you contributed within a wider team and what you learnt from that experience can provide a helpful stimulus.

The question, "what do you think you might learn from making a wider contribution to the team which will be relevant to your next job?" can provide a useful prompt for someone to think through how they would benefit from wider participation.

William had contributed to a plan for the setting up of a food bank in the local area. He asked Rachel to be part of the team organising the food bank working with representatives from other churches. William thought this would be an ideal opportunity for Rachel to be part of a wider team working with people from different backgrounds on a practical project. The experience helped Rachel develop her partnership skills with both the local authority and other voluntary organisations.

In practice

- See the long-term benefit of someone contributing within a wider team

- Enable them to be clear what learning they want out of this experience, and what contribution they can make

- See contributing as part of a wider team as an essential part of someone's personal development

- Ask periodically about what they are learning as a member of the team and how it is feeding back into the way they are tackling their individual responsibilities

- Ask what they are learning from different team members

39 CREATE MUTUAL SUPPORT STRUCTURES

WHEN SOMEONE IS able to create mutual support structures it is more likely that their learning will to be embedded over the longer term.

The idea

We are often at our most effective when we have alongside us someone who is fully committed to our success and who will tell us when we get it wrong. When I was the Director-General for Finance at the Department of Education and Employment I worked closely with another Board member. We were supportive to each other but also very challenging. We knew that we could work through issues in dialogue to get to a robust conclusion.

Asking someone what are the mutual support arrangements they want to put in place can prompt them to think about whose views do they trust and respect, and with whom can they have frank conversations which will lead to constructive learning.

When I lead workshops I encourage participants to work in pairs or threes with people they do not know and coach each other on how they tackle demanding situations. The resulting open dialogue often leads to the individuals meeting up again because they have found a way of being both supportive and challenging to someone in a similar type of role.

Encouraging people to keep refreshing their mutual support arrangements is important so that they are open to different people bringing varying perspectives and are not stuck in a routine of only hearing the same set of views.

William encouraged Rachel to meet with curates from other parishes. William encouraged Rachel to structure the conversation with the other curates so it became more like a learning set where they shared their experiences and worked through how they were going to tackle the different challenges they faced. Rachel found that there were a lot of parallels in the situations they were addressing.

Although she was initially apprehensive, she now looked forward to the meetings every six weeks with the two other curates. She knew she could talk through issues in an unfettered way and would always come out of the conversations with new ideas and a clear resolve about what she was going to do next.

In practice

- Share stories about mutual support arrangements that have worked well for you

- Legitimise people spending time supporting each other

- Encourage a balance between support and challenge with clear outcomes

- Encourage mutual support structures being refreshed with new combinations

- Encourage someone to articulate on a periodic basis how they have benefited from learning set-type arrangements

REINFORCE INDEPENDENCE OF MIND AND SPIRIT

THE OUTCOME OF a good coaching conversation is reinforced independence of mind and spirit. It is the exact opposite to creating dependence

The idea

Some critics are concerned that coaching-type conversations will create dependency. Good coaching conversations lead to exactly the opposite. My objective as a coach is to help someone reinforce their independence of mind and spirit. I want them to go out of a coaching conversation with a spring in their step knowing how they are going to handle the most demanding of situations. I want them to go out of the coaching conversation fresh, alert and buoyant feeling they have a coherent way forward.

Good coaching is about enabling someone to work through uncertainty and reach a point of clarity. It is about enabling them to move on from looking down to looking up with any spirit of despondency having been replaced by a spirit of adventure and hopefulness.

As the result of a good coaching conversation an individual will know their own mind and have an inner resolve. They will have thought through the link between their values and where they want to add value in a particular situation. Their sense of vision about what they want to achieve will be clearer and there will be a vitality in their approach which will carry them through tough times.

Reinforcing independence of mind and spirit is about finding the touch-points where conviction turns into action and a new confidence turns into courage.

Holding in your mind, "how can I reinforce independence of mind and spirit in this individual?" can provide you with an attitude of mind in the coaching conversation that enables them to go out of a conversation renewed, refreshed and reinvigorated. The risk of dependency is removed when you focus on setting people free to be the best they can be and enabling them to bring together all their life experience and values in the way they lead and influence others.

William knew that Rachel could be diffident and uncertain. His aim was to reinforce her independence of mind and spirit. He encouraged her to reflect on what she had learnt from those who had been independent minded. He invited her to reflect on what were the differences she would most like to see happen in her areas of responsibility. William encouraged her to be bold in setting out to build a team working with children and young people. Rachel felt increasingly emboldened because of William stressing the importance of her contribution and giving her the freedom to use independent action.

In practice

- See independence of mind and spirit as a plus and not a minus

- Encourage the development of new ideas and approaches

- Ask questions like, "if you were bold now, what would you do?"

- Be positive and not critical when being independent does not quite work

- Bring positive reinforcement when recognising constructive outcomes flowing from independence being used wisely

YOUR OWN LEARNING ABOUT COACHING

41 KEEP REVIEWING YOUR LEARNING

As YOU REVIEW your learning you crystallize and embed it.

The idea

As a leader or manager when you coach you are continually learning. Sometimes it is right to take stock and ask whether your approach is changing. Questions to ask yourself might be:

- Am I getting better at asking open questions?

- Am I varying my pace to take account of those I am working with?

- Am I maintaining full concentration and looking and sounding as if I am fully present in those conversations?

- What feedback am I getting about my coaching approach?

- What difference am I seeing in those I am working with: is there any noticeable change in their levels of competence and confidence?

- Am I increasingly confident about leaving space in a conversation to let the other person think?

- Am I willing to let the other person reach a conclusion and not feel that my job is to bring solutions?

It can be helpful to have two or three questions which you ask yourself on a regular basis and possibly to note down your own observations and see how they change over time.

David had been using a coaching approach increasingly with his people. He noticed that he was much less focused on giving people solutions. His pleasure came much more through enabling others to piece together different factors and reach their own view on next steps. David observed himself listening better and handling silences in conversations with greater ease than he had ever done before.

The question he would now often ask himself after a coaching conversation was, "what progress am I seeing in this individual and how best do I enable them to make the most of their undoubted potential?"

In practice

- Review your learning on a regular basis

- Have criteria you use to assess that learning

- Recognise whether you get more pleasure from enabling others to reach conclusions than bringing solutions yourself

- Observe how you are varying the pace to respond to others

- Celebrate your own learning

42 DEVELOP YOUR THINKING WITH TRUSTED OTHERS

THE SUPPORT AND encouragement of others who are also developing a coaching approach is likely to help you develop your coaching approach more quickly than doing it on your own.

The idea

When I work with teams I encourage them to use a coaching approach with each other and thereby begin to develop greater confidence in using a coaching approach with their peers. Often they begin to appreciate the value of focused coaching conversations with each other, especially where there is a mutual benefit in receiving coaching and giving coaching as part of a two-part conversation. I encourage them to reflect on how a coaching approach is working and to give feedback to each other about what type of approach and questions work well.

Encouraging teams to get to a point where members want to spend some time coaching each other provides them with a source of trusted advice as well as their own developing understanding.

If you and another colleague both decide that you want to develop more of a coaching approach it can be helpful to keep learning from each other and sharing your own experiences about what is working well or less well. Sharing good questions that prove to be effective can be an excellent way of taking your learning forward.

David was hesitant about whether he was using a coaching approach well. He was ambivalent about when to bring advice and firm direction into a conversation, and when to be more reflective in his tone and bring in a wider perspective. David talked with a colleague who had also received the same feedback as she tended to provide solutions too early.

Together they shared examples of how they were trying to use more of an enabling approach and learnt from each other's experience. As a consequence David became more confident in applying a coaching approach and was amused by his own willingness to be more restrained and hold back from offering solutions too quickly.

In practice

- Pair up with someone who is also developing more of a coaching approach

- Share experiences and examples and your learning from them

- Talk through how you will handle particular discussions

- Read the same book or article as a colleague and discuss your reactions and learning about what is applicable

- Be willing to adopt ideas about good questions and approaches that others suggest

WORK IN PARTNERSHIP WITH OTHERS

REFLECT ON WHO you can work in tandem with to enable an individual to develop their competence and confidence.

The idea

It is easier for someone to make progress if there are consistent, positive signals from the people they work with. The reinforcing effect of encouragement from a range of people on the same issue can be powerful.

An individual who is prone to speak too early and at too great a length in meetings may be surprisingly unaware of this tendency. Encouraging that individual to invite their colleagues and their staff to give them feedback after a meeting when they think they have intervened at too great a length can create a pattern of repeat messages. For this approach to work an individual has to be open in their request for feedback and then explicit in their thanks for the feedback, even when it has been critical.

If it is agreed in a performance appraisal that an individual needs to step up to take on responsibility more quickly in certain situations, it can help if a few of the people the individual works with know of this intent. The consequence can be that each of the colleagues is giving consistent and focused feedback.

If someone is permanently running late for meetings, your signalling of the importance of being prompt can be reinforced by agreement with close colleagues that they look disapproving if this individual is running late again. Working in partnership with others is about encouraging a group of people around someone to be consistently encouraging, and also willing to give consistent, overt messages when someone is not making the progress that they are expected to make and have the potential to make.

Sometimes there can be an implied partnership with significant others outside the office. If someone has a tendency to drift around a bit in the latter part of an afternoon asking them what stories they are going to read with their youngster that evening can prompt a greater sense of urgency about completing tasks and then going home.

One member of David's team needed to be more assertive in a particular area. The two of them agreed that they would invite another colleague to be ready to give feedback about when the contributions were suitably assertive. David built an expectation that there would be an open conversation following key meetings with a couple of other people about the nature of the contributions.

David worked openly with two or three colleagues to ensure that there was consistent feedback about when John was more assertive or not. John recognised what David was doing and was content with this reinforcement about when his approach was working.

In practice

- Think who you can work in partnership with to encourage the right type of behaviour adoption

- Be explicit about the value of building such a partnership

- Recognise the crucial role of feedback from junior staff who see the effects of someone's approach and behaviour most directly

- Start from an individual's willingness to take serious account of feedback

- Accept that the outcomes might not be entirely as you had initially predicted

44 RECOGNISE WHEN SPECIALIST HELP IS NEEDED

SOMETIMES INDIVIDUALS FACE problems that need specialist help and are not going to be solved by a coaching approach, be it through a sensitive manager or an experienced business coach.

The idea

Sometimes an individual would benefit from counselling or specialist medical support. If someone is caught in the grip of stress, a coaching approach will help at the margins but not solve the fundamental issues. When an individual has a complete mental block about tackling an issue, or is gripped in fear, then specialist help may be essential.

Some individuals are very open about the dilemmas they are facing and are ready to be pointed in the direction of specialist help, whereas others are intent on hiding their inability to cope. Sometimes people will look as if they are lapping up advice and coaching, but then do not move on. Often this is because there is an emotional struggle going on in someone's mind which is restricting their capacity to make any meaningful progress.

On two occasions, a few years apart, I had two individuals working for me who were always keen to make progress but never did. It subsequently became clear that both individuals were suffering from alcohol dependency and had developed a means of presenting an air of competence while below the surface they were caught in fear and used alcohol as their means of coping. On the second occasion I was unaware of the problem until a couple of years later when I heard that the individual had died of liver failure.

Enabling someone to face up to mental health issues, and encouraging them to find a way forward that they can take without feeling humiliated is important. As a good leader you are balancing your concern for the health of an organisation with that of individuals in it. You have a duty of care to those individuals who are struggling. Pointing them in the direction of specialist help can be the best thing for both them and the organisation.

David was conscious that Wendy kept repeating the same type of worries. Initially David thought that this was Wendy's way of talking the issue through, but increasingly David was conscious that Wendy was caught in a grip of fear. David encouraged Wendy to talk about the issue in a reflective way but seemed to be making little progress.

David organised for a specialist to come and lead a workshop for the team on stress management. He did not say to Wendy that he had her in mind when he set up the workshop. Wendy had been apprehensive about joining the workshop, but was fully absorbed with it and talked at the end about some practical steps she was going to take. Wendy recognised there was a broader issue she needed to address. David subsequently learnt that Wendy was seeing a counsellor and that the workshop on stress management had been an very important step enabling Wendy to be open to talk to a counsellor

In practice

It can be helpful to observe:

- If someone seems to be gripped by fear
- If they keep going around they same issue in a very emotional way

- When there are openings for discussion about the potential value of specialist help

- How the use of workshops on themes like stress management can help someone explore their own circumstances

- That most people at some time in their life will need specialist, medical help

KNOW YOUR LIMITATIONS

LIMITATIONS MIGHT BE about your own professional skills, but can also be about the circumstances which mean it would be inappropriate to go beyond certain boundaries

The idea

The tennis player who has a better forehand than a backhand will want to keep working on their backhand returns, but this tennis player will be mindful that they are at their most effective when they use forehand shots.

Each of us is conscious that we are likely to be more effective in coaching some people rather than others. Where there is a particular rapport, shared background or experience it can be easier to move into a coaching mode. We might have particular skills in building and developing relationships and, therefore, be good at coaching others to be able to be more influential. We might have had limited financial experience and, therefore, we are not going to be of much help in enabling someone to work through how they handle significant financial responsibilities.

When we are someone's line manager they may well not want to open up to us on some issues. Working in the same area as someone enables you to bring a perspective about what is needed for success to happen, but it can also create inhibitions and restrict the scope and freedom of coaching-type conversations. It is crucial that both parties feel that it is appropriate to be talking about a particular topic for coaching conversations to be successful. If there is a sense of embarrassment or unease the coaching will not be productive.

David was conscious that two of his managers would benefit from developing their presentation skills. David offered to do some coaching with both of them. Ann responded readily to this offer and was open with the dilemma she faced. David and Ann quickly got into some productive coaching conversations which enabled Ann to experiment with different approaches.

Ros was much less sure about whether she wanted to open to David about her concerns. David respected this unease and suggested that Ros might have a couple of conversations with another colleague elsewhere in the organisation. David stressed that there would be no feedback to him from these conversations. Ros accepted this alternative offer which provided her with a secure space to think through and develop her approach to giving presentations.

In practice

- Recognise your areas of expertise and your less strong areas

- Be honest to yourself about the areas where you coach well and where you are less effective

- Never be offended if someone would prefer to have a coaching conversation with someone other than you

- Agree what the boundaries are in coaching conversations and articulate the importance of confidentiality

- Recognise when you have the type of rapport with someone which means coaching can be productive, and also when the type of rapport is not strong enough to allow the type of openness and frankness that allows coaching conversations to be at their most effective

46 USE AN EXTERNAL BUSINESS COACH WISELY

Bringing in an external business coach can provide an external perspective and a confidential space for an individual or team to work through options in an unfettered way.

The idea

Bringing a coaching approach as a leader or manager can enable an individual or team to progress so far. But there are moments when bringing in an external business coach can help ensure there is a step change in someone's contribution. A good business coach can bring a wider perspective from a range of different contexts.

A good business coach will have significant experience in leadership themselves and will have coached leaders in a variety of different sectors. The business coach will help bring precision to an individual's articulation of their own story and the way they look to address future opportunities.

An external coach can be particularly useful when an individual is:

- Looking to take on bigger responsibilities

- Leading a change programme where progress needs to be made quickly

- Needing to step up in the way they lead

- Handling situations where there is conflict and a way through needs to be found that builds a new sense of purpose and coherence

Using an external business coach can be valuable when a team has lost its way and needs to reshape its purpose with more clarity about how members of the team are going to work effectively together going forward.

A good business coach will enable individuals, to clarify their own understanding of their competences, be more confident about how they are going to step up to take on bigger responsibilities, be clearer how they are going to have the impact they want in different spheres and, bring a more coherent and authentic approach to their leadership responsibilities.

Leo invited Mary to meet an external coach as she was taking on a much wider responsibility. Leo was happy to mentor Mary, but thought she would benefit from coaching conversations with someone who had wider and more senior business experience. Mary overcame her initial scepticism and found the coaching conversations hugely rewarding.

Mary was able to talk options through with the coach in an unfettered way. She looked forward to the coaching conversations knowing that by the end of them she would have worked out a strategy for dealing with the major objectives she was now taking forward. Leo checked in with Mary occasionally but trusted the coach to make the best possible use of the time

In practice

- See an external business coach as a complement to the coaching work you do

- Draw in an external coach who has sound, senior level experience

- Be mindful of finding the right chemistry between coach and coachee

- Allow the coaching relationship to flow without being impaired by too much curiosity, once the objectives have been set

- Review the effectiveness of the coaching relationship on a periodic basis

47 UNDERSTAND YOUR OWN EMOTIONS

YOUR EMOTIONS CAN provide you with very valuable data, but can sometimes get in the way.

The idea

When you are in coaching mode sometimes your emotions can get in the way. You want to see yourself as a good coach and, therefore, will be looking for approval. You want the person you are working with to say nice things about your coaching approach on a regular basis. But your aim is to get the individual thinking hard rather than praising you.

There can be a risk that if there is silence you feel that you are not doing your job properly, but silence can mean thoughtfulness with someone engaged in working through an issue. You want the individual to be focused on what they are going to do next and not to be reflecting on the quality of your coaching.

Sometimes you might have an emotional reaction that someone is in danger of making a wrong decision. Your emotional reaction might be to dive in and tell them they ought to change course. But it is their life and not yours. Your role is to pose questions about what they are considering and enable them to work through the consequences. If your emotions are too obvious it can distort the conversation and the capacity for somebody to work through issues in a calm and reflective way.

On the other hand your emotions are valuable data about what is going on in a particular situation and can give you insight which can enable you to help bring clarity to what might otherwise be a confusing situation.

Mary kept coming up with radical, new ideas for making the team more effective. Inside Leo cringed at a number of these ideas and thought they could be counter-productive. Leo did not want to dampen Mary's enthusiasm. Leo provided space for Mary to talk through the different options and showed complete absorption in the different options.

Leo asked questions about the consequences of the different possibilities. Leo did say that a couple of the ideas were non-starters, but deliberately did not express a view on most of the possibilities. She stayed focused on enabling Mary to work through the implications of the ideas.

In practice

- Watch to see if your emotions are distorting your own reactions

- Be mindful if your emotional reactions are obvious and having a counter-productive effect on the person you are working with

- See your emotions as giving you valuable insights

- Understand when your pride might be being hurt because the individual is focusing on their issues rather than thanking you for the coaching

- Recognise the patterns in your own emotions

48 RECOGNISE WHEN YOUR JOB IS DONE

IT IS IMPORTANT to recognise when coaching work is complete and when both you and the coachee should move on in the working relationship.

The idea

It can be much more difficult to end a coaching relationship than to start it. When time and effort has gone in to building a productive pattern of coaching conversations with an individual there is a natural desire to keep it going. Ending a coaching relationship can feel like a bereavement and can be quite emotional.

When there are clear objectives for a set of coaching conversations it is helpful to review in a dispassionate way the extent to which those objectives have been met. A review point provides a good basis for either bringing coaching conversations to a conclusion or starting a next phase with a new set of objectives.

As a manager you may be building a coaching style into the way you manage your people. You may deliberately use the style on some issues an individual is facing and then apply that approach on subsequent issues. It is an important part of the contracting that both parties agree when it is valuable to be using a coaching approach. If someone asks specifically for you to use a coaching approach on future issues it shows that the relationship is maturing for both of you.

As a leader of a large group of people you may decide that you are going to use a coaching approach in a differentiated way focused with individuals who are at particular points in their development.

You might then deliberately have a couple of conversations with one individual leaving them with a clear set of learning and action points, and then move your focus to other people in the team.

Leo recognised that Norman was finding it hard to build a coherent team focused on the same objectives. Leo offered to work with Norman over the next couple of months to help him clarify objectives and build a more coherent team. They agreed to meet every couple of weeks over the two-month period.

At the end of the fourth conversation Leo asked Norman to set out his own next steps having built a greater sense of shared endeavour amongst his team. This was a natural point to conclude this set of focused coaching conversations. Norman knew that he could talk to Leo if he wanted to subsequently, but recognised that it was now for him to take forward next steps having developed a clear plan in conversation with Leo.

In practice

- Be clear on time-bound objectives

- Review progress in an objective way

- Bring a sequence of coaching conversations to an end point in a constructive and unemotional way

- Recognise that ending one coaching conversation provides an opportunity for starting up a set of coaching conversations with someone else

- Include review points if a coaching conversation continues over a long period

CELEBRATE YOUR OWN JOURNEY AS A COACH

As you recognise the progress you are making as a coach you embed that learning and become even more effective as a coach.

The idea

You are learning all the time. It is only as you look back that you see the progress you have made. As you become more comfortable asking open-ended questions and leaving silences you become more comfortable in yourself as a coach.

It is right to celebrate in yourself that you are much more relaxed in coaching conversations, and that you can spot the right question more easily. You might begin to observe in yourself a greater ability to draw comparisons or use analogies. You might observe that the person you are working with is more willing to open up in conversation and able to link together their professional and personal experiences. They are less anguished in handling their emotions and able to sit outside themselves more readily and appreciate what is going on in interrelating their thoughts and emotions.

As you become more experienced using a coaching approach you can celebrate the energy you see in the people you are working with and their ability to reach their own conclusions more easily about the way forward. It can be celebrated that they are looking to you to help enable them to work through issues, rather than to tell them what to do. Your role has fairly seamlessly moved from being directive to gentle steering and being a stimulus to thinking in new ways.

Leo felt she was able to stand back increasingly and observe what her staff was doing rather than tell them what to do next. She understood more about what made them enthusiastic and what dampened their energy. She more readily appreciated how best to offer comment so that it got a positive and not a defensive reaction.

Leo felt she could sit more lightly to her responsibilities and not feel she had to be on top of every piece of work every day. She felt better as a consequence of bringing more of a coaching approach. Her staff felt that they were being trusted. Their commitment was higher. There was a much greater buzz in the office with Leo finding herself smiling more often.

In practice

- See the progress made when coaching others

- Recognise how you are asking questions differently and using silence more effectively

- Enjoy the success of those you have been working with and recognise your part in their development

- See your journey as continuous as you use more varied examples and different analogies in your coaching conversations

- See your coaching skills as equally applicable inside and outside a work environment

50 · LOOK FORWARD WITH EXPECTATION

KEEP SEEING DIFFERENT ways in which you can use your coaching approach at work and outside work.

The idea

Coaching people well is a skill you can use for the rest of your life. Coaching is about enabling those you are with at every stage of life to understand the context they are in and to make the difference they want to make in subsequent phases of life and work. As you coach someone you enable them to develop skills for the short-term and the long-term. Encouraging them to cast forward those skills into the future can help build a confidence that they can influence a wide-range of people for good.

Coaching is partly about enabling people to live their values well in order to build on the good and wholesome, and to address what is evil and insidious in any organisation. Where you have enabled individuals to be more confident in addressing destructive behaviour you are helping to equip them to be forces for good as they progress through an organisation or move elsewhere.

The outcome of coaching conversations is not just greater efficiency and effectiveness. It is about a commitment to improve the way values are lived in any sphere. Your contribution can be to enable another generation to overcome prejudice, to ensure fairness and integrity, and to create a culture where there is mutual respect, with the qualities in people developed and applied to the full. Your contribution can enable someone to fulfil their potential and be a profound influence for good in building future organisations that are responsive, supportive, honest, wholesome and supportive.

Leo was delighted by the progress of the young people with potential in her organisation. She recognised their energy and admired their desire to make a difference. She saw teams working co-operatively together with a strong sense of mutual support.

Leo was delighted that financial greed was not part of the culture and that status was much less important than competence. She delighted in the progress of those she had worked with. She looked forward in expectation about the impact of these young leaders in the years ahead.

In practice

- Enable people to link together their ambitions and values

- Enable developing leaders to see how they can create organisations where greed, prejudice and possessiveness play no part

- Recognise your role in raising expectations about quality, building on the good and diminishing the evil and the insidious

- Encourage a hopefulness about what can be achieved and an expectation that 'all things can work together for good'

- Encourage a belief that new life and energy is possible in even the darkest of situations

PART 2

APPLYING COACHING IN SPECIFIC CONTEXTS

ENSURING HIGH QUALITY OUTCOMES

CREATING BOLD EXPECTATIONS ABOUT OUTCOMES

A KEY STARTING point is creating bold expectations about outcomes that are both stretching and within the bounds of realism.

The idea

Creating bold expectations is about stimulating an individual's or team's mental and emotional energy. Outcomes to be effective need to be tangible and preferably visual as a focus for intellectual and emotional drive. The outcome might be a product that is manufactured, an IT system that is installed, a Bill that becomes an Act of Parliament or a report that is published.

Enabling individuals or teams to 'see' what a product will be like helps create the expectation that a product can be developed and delivered successfully. But the expectation needs to be realistic. It helps if you can point to previous examples of success by either the same team or other teams.

If a bold expectation is all about rhetoric, it will appear empty. What is crucial is that individuals believe that good quality outcomes can be attained and that they can see a part that they can play in delivering those outcomes. For expectations about outcomes to be credible, you as leader need to be able to demonstrate your full commitment to them and your willingness to make some personal sacrifices in order to deliver those outcomes. Others need to see your commitment and your willingness to bring an element of vicariousness in order to ensure those outcomes are delivered.

Harvey had been given responsibility for overseeing the preparation of a Parliamentary Bill covering an element of education reform. He knew he would be very dependent on his team. Harvey built a clear understanding about the purpose of the Bill and the contribution of each member of the team to delivering its passage through Parliament. He drew from his own previous experience to illustrate what was possible.

Harvey drew from examples of pieces of legislation which had been hard work to deliver and had created outcomes that had been beneficial for many children and families. Harvey had a clear story he told on a number of occasions about the outcomes recognising that members of the team would grasp the process at different rates. It was crucial he did not assume everyone had the same quickness of mind and enthusiasm for this project.

In practice

- Create bold expectations about outcomes that are clear, unambiguous and memorable
- Enable your outcomes to be as visual as possible and repeat the narrative on a regular basis
- Recognise that different people will grasp the outcomes at different speeds
- Demonstrate your commitment through showing what you will personally sacrifice to reach this outcome
- Ensure that your narrative has a ring of reality about it

52 BUILDING A PATHWAY TO SUCCESS

BUILDING A PATHWAY to success with clear milestones along the way provides a reassurance that an outcome is possible

The idea

Some prefer to see a clear pathway ahead with obvious, regular milestones. For others a way ahead that is attractive is broader with more scope for individual freedom and choice along the way. For some a narrow pathway works best, while for others a broad and elastic highway is what brings out the best in them.

For some the route map is specific and followed meticulously: the equivalent of the ordnance survey map is carried around the neck and is consulted frequently. For others a quick glance at the map at the start gives an overall sense of direction, and then the map is only consulted if there appears to be something unusal in the way the journey unfolds.

Sometimes, where someone is doing a piece of individual research the pathway to success is very individualistic, but most people will be conscious of other people on the pathway, either as part of the same team or on a similar journey. Being able to see others on the same pathway can help renew the resolve that this is the right direction.

Travelling on a route which others have been on before provides a confidence that the pathway is going to an appropriate destination. The leader as coach is pointing the way and recognising the amount of detail and instruction that different people need, alongside the importance of enabling them to make their own decisions about the precise route-way and speed of travel.

Harvey explained carefully to the team the different steps in putting a Bill through Parliament. He was meticulous in explaining the stages: he invited members of the team to talk to other colleagues who had been involved in putting legislation through Parliament.

In a two-hour, open session Harvey invited members of the team to think about how best they would work together in order to deliver the necessary timetable. Harvey was prescriptive about the fixed points, but wanted individuals in the team to reach their own conclusions about how they were going to use their time and energy and how they were going to best work together.

In practice

- Describe the pathway to success with energy and in a way that people can visualise

- Describe elements of the pathway that might be a narrow route or a broad highway in order to catch the imagination of different people in the team

- Create a clear understanding of the milestones along the way

- Build an acceptance that this is a doable pathway, but one that will have its surprises

- Recognise the pace that is needed to reach the destination, and also the pace to which individuals are willing and able to travel

53 FOSTERING AN AWARENESS OF RISKS

FOSTERING AN AWARENESS of risks and knowing what the contingent plans are to handle those risks is crucial to the success of any venture.

The idea

The good leader is both building bold expectations about the pathway to success, and fostering an awareness of risks and ensuring the preparation of contingent arrangements.

The walker is addressing the risk of rain by carrying a waterproof jacket and trousers in their backpack. They are countering the risk of rough ground by wearing tough boots. On wet rocks they may be acknowledging the risk of slipping by using a mountain pole. For the long-distance walker it is folly to ignore the risks. Carrying an extra bottle of water or a block of Kendal mint cake provides a reassurance that if you get lost, emergency rations are available.

Inviting individuals or a team to think through what are the risks they face and what are the contingent arrangements that need to be put in place is never wasted. But there does need to be a proportionality about the risks. On a long walk in the summer it is theoretically possible that the temperature might drop 15° but the unlikely possibility means you are not likely to carry a thick sweater. But even on the sunniest of days there is the risk of a shower, so carrying a waterproof jacket in the back-pack is almost invariably going to be sensible, contingent planning.

Spending time with individuals or teams exploring risks and looking at their likelihood and the consequence is never wasted.

What is important is ensuring that this exploration does not destroy the sense of bold expectation about the pathway to success. Having explored the risks there might be a decision to change the timing: e.g. to move the walk up the mountain to another day. But the exploration of risks is not intended to kill off the aspiration. It is about keeping in balance the boldness of expectation alongside realism about the awareness of risks.

Harvey talked with the team about the risks involved in putting the Bill through Parliament. The Parliamentary draughtsman will have other Bills to prepare and will not be focused just on this Bill. Government Ministers might be clear now about what they want in the Bill, but then be lobbied successfully by different groups and decide to change their mind. The Parliamentary process will always produce the unexpected with political parties and individuals not being predictable.

Events and news stories may change the climate of opinion which means that a step which looked sensible in theory might be creating emotive reactions which mean that the Bill is going to need amending. Harvey got his team to think through all these risks. He wanted to encourage in the team both focus and flexibility, so that they could be both single-minded and adapt their approach when needed.

In practice

- Draw on your own experience of defining and handling risks in similar, past situations

- Set out the risks in a dispassionate way and enable others to think through how the risks might be handled

- Create an expectation that there will always be surprises and encourage a response that is one of curiosity rather than doom

- Describe the handling of risks, as a key part of learning for each individual

- Ensure that looking at risks informs and does not necessarily dampen expectations

54 KNOWING HOW PROGRESS WILL BE MEASURED

IF A PROJECT is to be successful, clarity about how progress is to be measured and effective communication about progress is important in maintaining motivation.

The idea

Organisations that encourage feedback are often responsive and adaptable. Feedback from clients and customers may say as much about them as it does about us, but it always contains nuggets of truth. Feedback from our staff may hurt when we feel that our efforts are not as appreciated as we would like, or that our intentions seem to be misunderstood. But perception is reality, so if the feedback is that we need to improve in certain areas, then it is folly to ignore that advice.

In healthy organisations feedback is a two-way process. Our boss may or may not invite feedback and jumping in boldly with critical feedback may not be the best way of trying to influence them. Feedback is irrelevant if it is dismissed without proper consideration.

Before giving feedback we need to try and create an atmosphere in which feedback is invited and welcomed. A leader can be asked whether they would find feedback helpful. Provided there is a good balance between positive and development comments, most people will be happy to receive feedback if it is given in a constructive way.

Feedback that is sensitive to the context someone is in and is steering them in a particular direction can have a long-term, positive impact. If you are known as someone who gives good quality feedback, those who want to improve their contribution will seek your feedback.

Liz was hesitant about giving feedback to her boss after he had chaired a meeting that went badly wrong. She decided not to tackle this head-on, but she did want to raise the subject with her boss. In a private conversation, Liz asked her boss how he thought the meeting had gone. When she got a non-committal answer, Liz asked gently whether he might handle a future meeting in a slightly different way. Her boss admitted that the meeting had not been perfect and asked Liz for any suggestions. This gave her the opportunity to express some views. She did not have to press her case too hard as her boss clearly accepted that the next meeting needed to be conducted differently.

In practice

- Build clarity about how progress will be measured so there is little chance of ambiguity

- Recognise that different people will respond to different ways of assessing progress

- Enable individuals and the team to recognise that key senior players will want different types of progress

- Ensure progress is measured if you have said it will be measured, or you will not be believed next time you say that measurement is important

- Allow your own progress to be measured and recognise what you have learnt from the results of the assessment

55 BRINGING CLARITY OF ROLE

ENSURING CLARITY OF role means energy can be used to best effect and minimises friction.

The idea

Part of your role as the leader is to ensure clarity of role so that individuals are clear about the expectations of them and their contribution to the overall venture. But you will want that clarity of role to be adaptable as individuals develop and are able to take on more responsibilities, and as circumstances change.

Clarity of role is not just about the type of activity. It can also be about perspective and attitude of mind. Individuals within a team will each bring their own technical competence and experience, but it can be well worth legitimising their role in terms of the wider perspective they bring. You might task one person with being the visionary, another to look from the perspective of the customer, another to bring a particular focus on efficiency and effectiveness, and another to look in particular at risks and how they are handled.

In a team that is working well individuals will switch roles from time to time to broaden their own experience, and so that the perspective they bring from one role can be applied in another activity.

A leader who is coaching an individual well enables them to move from role to role in a way that keeps maximizing their learning. The leader who is coaching their team well continues to widen the competences of members of the team so that the overall team becomes more adaptable and stronger.

Harvey had a small team committed to supporting Ministers in taking the Bill through Parliament successfully. They each had their particular area of responsibility. Harvey was conscious that when notes on amendments and speaking notes had to be prepared at speed, it was important to split the role between the person who did the first draft and someone who checked through each speaking role to ensure that in the haste errors were not being made. The reader was expected to look at what phrases could be misinterpreted and whether language needed to be tightened.

When the going got tough, individual members of the team knew when it was their responsibility to encourage and help sustain other members of the team. One member of the team was asked to keep a particular eye on how different groups were responding to the Bill as it went through Parliament. When the Bill moved from the House of Commons to the House of Lords, Harvey switched some of the roles to enable individuals to keep widening their experience, and so they kept fresh.

In practice

- Be clear about respective roles, but don't cast them in stone

- Look at roles not only in terms of task, but also in terms of wider perspective and aspects to look out for

- Be mindful when roles can be inter-changeable and how they might evolve over time

- When roles do change ensure that communication is clear

- Allow roles to evolve over time in a planned and adaptable rather than a random way

ENABLING SOMEONE TO STEP UP IN RESPONSIBILITY

56 CREATING A PICTURE OF SUCCESS

CREATING A PICTURE of success turns an aspiration into something that is attainable, even if challenging.

The idea

When someone knows they have to step up in responsibility it can be daunting. The outward appearance might be one of confidence, but the inner reality may be very different. Sometimes success can feel like an impossible dream. The obstacles on the way can appear massive and almost overwhelming.

For others picturing success is straightforward. They have been frustrated for a while in their current role and can readily see what needs to be done. For these individuals the role of leader as coach is to help them shape that picture of success. It is not about helping them develop the confidence to believe success is attainable as their confidence is already strong.

For those who are daunted by the prospect of stepping up in responsibility your role can be to help them put together the jigsaw so they see how all the parts fit together. Success comes through seeing the inter-relationships and having the patience to put one piece of the jigsaw on the board at a time.

Stepping up in responsibility is also about leaving stuff behind. Your role might be to help someone recognise what they need to leave behind in order to move out of their comfort zone, and be liberated from previous assumptions and approaches that have been fundamental for them. Enabling someone to move away from dealing with the detail into seeing the inter-relationships and the bigger picture can provide a new freedom enabling them to be excited about the prospect of stepping up.

Janette felt mesmerized by the prospect of becoming a team leader. She knew she wanted to take on this responsibility and had been selected through a tough competition. But there was a hesitancy which she did not fully understand. Every time she began to think about what success would look like in the role she became anxious. Her boss sensed this apprehension and began to work with her on what were the key outcomes that the team needed to deliver and what would be Janette's contribution to that success.

Janette's boss encouraged her to think of what success would look like in different areas. Her boss then invited Janette to stand back and look at what excited her and what daunted her about delivering on the range of responsibilities. Once Janette could see what success looked like, her confidence began to rise and she was clear that the job was possible. She even allowed herself to begin to feel a touch of excitement.

In practice

- Sense how daunted an individual is about stepping up in responsibility

- Encourage them to see the job as an interlocking jigsaw focusing on the individual pieces and then on the whole picture

- Encourage someone to be clear what will excite them about the opportunities going forward

- Encourage them to describe, in their own language, what success would look like

- Suggest that individuals create a visual picture of success

57 DRAWING FROM PREVIOUS STEPS

THE MORE SOMEONE sees stepping up into new responsibility as a continuation of previous stepping up, the easier it will be to pace that progression effectively.

The idea

The walk up Jacob's Ladder in the English Peak District is a long, tough climb. The steps are not regular and in wet weather can be slippery. Half-way up, when you look back, you see the progress you have made. Looking forward you know it is possible to build on that progress and ensure the destination is reached. Enabling an individual to see their progression and how far they have climbed enables them to focus the energy for next steps. If rough steps have been successfully handled before, they can be handled again.

Seeing stepping up into responsibility as a sequence of attainable steps is far less daunting than seeing it as a scree slope that has to be scrambled up. Agreeing with an individual their practical, next steps in terms of both tasks and confidence can help an individual structure their intent to step up in responsibility.

Encouraging someone to use the visual analogy of steps and potentially construct a diagram setting out their steps can provide a helpful means of enabling steady and progressive progress.

When Janette expressed unease about taking on some of her new responsibilities her boss encouraged her to reflect on how she had handled her previous promotion. Janette reflected on the previous steps she had taken and what had motivated her and encouraged her. Janette recognised how important the belief in her of her parents and a couple of close friends was. Remembering how she had stepped up in her previous role reminded her what type of support she needed and enabled her to recall how her confidence had grown in steps as she had mastered new elements of the responsibility.

Looking backwards and forwards as a continuum helped Janette be confident about taking on new responsibilities. She knew that she needed to talk through steps with a couple of people who knew her well. Janette knew that she would need to take a deep breath and be more assertive in some situations. She recognised, most of the time that this was all in the realm of the doable. When there were flashes of doubt she told herself to remember the steps she had already taken successfully.

In practice

- Share elements of your journey that might be relevant to those stepping up

- Encourage individuals to take stock of progress so far and use that as a source of strength

- Enable individuals to construct a sequence of practical steps going forward

- Encourage people to visualise the type of steps they are about to walk on

- Invite individuals to reflect on what will enable them to step lightly rather than wearily

58 BUILDING ON STRENGTHS

ENCOURAGING INDIVIDUALS TO always start with strengths and build on them provides a much surer foundation than starting off with weaknesses and what needs to change.

The idea

Most people recognise their weaknesses much more readily than their strengths. Often the preoccupation is how can the weaknesses be reduced or hidden. When we are observing others it is often easier to focus on their limitations than on their strengths.

Enabling an individual to focus on the strengths they bring and how valuable they are going to be as they step up into bigger responsibilities is always the right place to start. They will have been appointed to a job because others recognise strengths in them. Enabling an individual to believe in their own strengths and build on them is perhaps the greatest contribution that a boss can make.

Enabling someone to articulate the strengths that they use outside of work can help widen the repertoire within the work context. Encouraging a parent to think about the capabilities they use in organising a complicated life and bringing up children can remind them of strengths that are deployable in other contexts too. Helping somebody to crystallize what are the strengths they use in activities in the wider community or in their wider families can provide new confidence in the ability to tackle different situations well.

The simple exercise of inviting someone to reflect on their own strengths, on how family members would describe their strengths and on how colleagues would describe their strengths, can enable someone to build a narrative about their generic capabilities which will enable them to bring inner confidence to responsibilities they take on.

Janette was a superb organiser in her personal life. She used her time and energy well in managing home life with two children and a husband in a busy role. She set clear expectations and built partnerships with other parents. She knew how to negotiate with her children. Janette had never thought about the transferability of these skills into the work environment until a friend described her as brilliant in balancing different priorities.

When Janette's boss encouraged her to think about what were the strengths she brought from family life into her work the positive comment from her friend popped up in her memory. Recognising the confidence she was able to use in organising her home life, she told herself this was a strength that was going to be immensely valuable as she took on new responsibilities at work.

In practice

Central to enabling someone to step up is to:

- Provide space for them to articulate their strengths

- Encourage them to use strengths from other spheres of their life

- Encourage them to visualise the transferability of their strengths from one area of their life to another

- Stretch their thinking about how their strengths can be applied in new ways

- Celebrate strengths as the bedrock on which they can now build

59 RECOGNISING WHAT 'BEING GROWN UP' MEANS

BEING GROWN UP is about accepting responsibility, treating people like equals and not being a dependant child any more.

The idea

Encouraging individuals to recognise when they are acting as a child and when as an adult can help them differentiate their attitudes and behaviours. Bringing the curiosity and freshness of the child is often a valuable starting point. But encouraging someone to move on from dependency on others and be willing to explore beyond the comfortable is a key element of enabling someone to grow up.

Encouraging someone to think about what type of 'adult to adult' conversation would they like to have with someone can help them be more confident and assertive in dealing with people they might naturally feel deferential towards. Seeing an adult to adult conversation as an open exchange of ideas and views which is not inhibited by status can lead to a sense of emancipation and freedom.

The question, "in this context do you feel like a grown up?" can help someone express their emotions about a situation and thereby be in a better position to recognise and handle those emotions. The question, "what will help you grow up into this space even more?" can sound a provocative question but can often provide the stimulus to thinking hard about what needs to happen next.

Janette, in the company of some of her colleagues, felt like curling up in a corner. She felt like a seven-year-old in their presence and not like a 37-year-old. Janette knew that this retreat to childhood attitudes was unhelpful. She observed herself in order to recognise the pattern and what set off this reaction. Janette spotted that if she rushed into a conversation late she could revert to this child-like emotion.

Janette knew she had to enter a conversation in a measured and paced way. She had to sit up straight, collect her thoughts and then intervene slowly and firmly. Once she had developed a technique that worked for her, she felt much more an adult with less risk of a reversion to childhood behaviour. Janette used as her mantra, as she entered this new role, "I am a grown up now". Repeating this mantra on a regular basis helped her be confident and assertive.

In practice

- Invite someone to reflect on what is the grown up behaviour they have seen others exhibit in a particular situations

- Talk through what does grown up behaviour mean in a particular situation

- Be explicit about the risks of acting like a child rather than as an adult

- Encourage someone to think through what would help them act in a grown up way in different situations

- Recognise that encouraging the excitement of childhood curiosity and freshness is also important

60 | TAKING BIGGER STRIDES

TAKING A LOT of short strides can be tiring and boring. Enabling someone to take bigger strides helps with both confidence and productivity.

The idea

When a pathway is slippery shorter strides are necessary to retain balance. When a path is rough and uneven the most productive way of walking is using long strides. When the pathway is smooth and you take clear long strides, the destination is reached quicker.

Encouraging someone to talk about what type of strides they are taking in a particular activity can enable them to reflect on their level of confidence, what sort of rhythm they are in, what might be affecting their equilibrium and what sort of pace they are comfortable with in moving forward. Inviting them to think about what type of strides they are taking in different aspects of their responsibilities can help them interlink both their progress and their attitude of mind. It can lead to a fruitful conversation about what is affecting their balance and how best do they counteract the risk of slipping or falling.

Asking the question, "what will enable you to lengthen your stride?" can prompt a fruitful conversation on confidence and competence. Lengthening the stride is dependent on clarity about the forward direction, the commitment to reach a destination and an efficient co-ordination of mind and body. Lengthening the stride results from focus and efficiency in the use of energy. Sometimes if a stride is too long there is a risk of over balancing and using energy inefficiently rather than smoothly.

Janette was encouraged by her boss to think about the type of strides she wanted to take in her new role and what would enable her to take longer strides. Janette talked about the need for her to be clear on the pathway ahead and what might cause her to slip.

Janette wanted to be confident in the people she was following and have confidence in the strides of the people around her. Janette could visualise the rhythm as she took strides in her job. This brought a smile to her face and helped her visualise how she would do this job well going forward.

In practice

- Use the visual image of, 'what type of strides are you wanting to take?'

- Encourage someone to think about how they might vary their stride

- Use questions like, "what will help you lengthen your stride?"

- Ask about what will put you off your stride and how might you handle that

- Encourage someone to see different lengths of stride as appropriate in different contexts

- See stride length as a means of pacing different types of situation

BUILDING STRONG PARTNERSHIPS

RECOGNISING SHARED INTERESTS

RECOGNISING SHARED INTERESTS and scope for a win/win is central to building a partnership that is going to hold together successfully.

The idea

Any successful, human partnership involves both rational reason and emotional commitment. There has to be a focus on a shared interest for a partnership or a coalition to survive. There needs to be a hard edge about the success that is sought and the consequences of giving up on that shared interest.

When there is the possibility of working in partnership the initial reaction will be dictated by emotions as much as logic. Do I want to work with that person? Will there be an element of fun or will it be boring? Will we get in each others' way?

The leader as coach seeks to enable somebody to take account of their emotional reactions and to look beyond those reactions to the hard edge of what is the mutual interest and potential gain from working together. You may want to facilitate an initial meeting, or to encourage the different parties to meet up and talk about the shared interests. When there is a risk of a response of wanting to sit on the side and 'not wanting to play' your reaction might be one of irritation, when mild amusement might be a more helpful observation.

To some shared interest is obvious: the architect has to work with the engineer, and the doctor has to work with the nurse. But for some the shared interest may not be quite as obvious. But the young barrister does need to work with the Court staff, and the marketing expert does need to work with the designer if they are going to produce a successful product.

Gillian felt she had little to learn from Harry. Gillian was a successful medical consultant who was dismissive of the work of hospital administrators. When she first met Harry she ignored him and thought of him as a minor bureaucrat. When Gillian could not get her way in ensuring some repair work was done to one of the operating suites, she stomped around and wrote strongly worded e-mails that were interpreted as rude.

Gillian dismissed any suggestion that Harry might be able to help her, but as her frustration got deeper she was willing to explore any route forward. Eventually, she asked to have a word with Harry who quietly set out a possible approach. Harry's tone calmed Gillian down. Reluctantly she accepted Harry's advice to show less irritation in the way she set out her arguments which led to a good outcome. Gillian, somewhat reluctantly, had begun to appreciate working in partnership with Harry.

In practice

When encouraging people to work in partnership remember to:

- Role model partnership working yourself

- Point out the benefits of partnership working simply and clearly

- Recognise when is the type of moment when proud individuals are willing to work in partnership

- Tell stories about where partnership has worked well

- Encourage people to think and talk openly about what might be shared interests going forward

BUILDING COMMON PURPOSE

UNLESS PARTNERSHIP HAS a common purpose it will rapidly dissipate. The common purpose needs to be well understood and regularly reiterated.

The idea

Members of the sports team that are working well together will be able to describe a clear narrative about why they work well together and what they are seeking to achieve. Any partnership needs a narrative that is believed in and engages the listener. The narrative needs to be told with conviction and credibility. A narrative that drifts off will send people to sleep. The good narrative needs clarity of outcomes and a punch-line which catches the imagination and is believable.

Sometimes the common purpose is obvious. For a football team it is to score goals. Sometimes individuals will focus on their own particular purpose rather than the goal of the organisation. Enabling individuals to see their goal as the collective outcome rather than just the individual outcomes will lead to a much more robust sense of common purpose. If an organisation is going to withstand change effectively, having a clear narrative and common purpose is not an optional extra: it is an essential element of success.

Gillian wanted to press hard for more capital investment in operating theatres but was unsure what steps to take. Harry recognised that as the key administrator he needed to build common purpose with Gillian and help coach her so that she did not behave like a 'bull in a China shop'. Harry was insistent that Gillian think carefully who she was going to influence and how she was going to build momentum for further investment in operating theatre capacity.

Harry was persistent in saying that evidence was more important than rhetoric. They put a narrative together about the benefits of the investment and the demand they would be meeting. Gillian reluctantly accepted that she needed some of Harry's diplomatic skills and acquiesced in being coached by him. Harry knew he had to use time efficiently with Gillian, but recognised he could press his point hard because Gillian was so committed to this investment that she was prepared to modify her approach in the light of Harry's advice.

In practice

- Build clarity about the outcomes
- Spend time building a shared narrative
- Keep using and developing the narrative making it ever more visual and populating it with stories
- Recognise that building common purpose will not always be straightforward when emotions get in the way
- Ensure there are regular reviews of how well a partnership is approaching the common purpose and to what extent the narrative is consistent

63 KNOWING WHERE YOUR FIXED POINTS ARE

BEING CLEAR ON the fixed points, alongside the scope for adaptability, is more likely to lead to successful outcomes than complete fluidity.

The idea

The leader as coach seeks to enable the individual to balance what is fixed alongside what is adaptable. Bringing clarity about what is fixed gives a basis on which a partnership can work. The fixed points may be about the size of the funding, or the timescale, or the involvement of different parties. The more explicit and understood the fixed points are the better. If the fixed points are unsaid they can become the source of suspicion. The good leader will want to ensure that the fixed points in terms of outcomes and behaviours are visible and discussed.

Any partnership needs fixed review points when the health of the partnership is assessed and future progress defined. The leader who seeks to build a strong partnership can use a coaching style in asking questions, setting expectations and reviewing progress. These can be encouraging, constructive discussions enabling people to think through whether sticking to a particular line is unnecessary stubbornness or an essential prerequisite of success.

Gillian was always trying to push the boundaries. She wanted more resources and more favourable treatment. Harry had to push back frequently and be explicit about the restrictions that inevitably had to constrain Gillian's freedom of actions. There were not unlimited recourses. Staff could not be recruited at a week's notice. Harry was firm and clear in describing fixed points and drawing attention to when he saw Gillian acting unreasonably. At the same time Harry respected Gillian's verve and energy. He had no wish to dampen her enthusiasm. It was about steering Gillian into the most productive direction.

Harry got Gillian to think how to accommodate the interests of other consultants in order to reach a stronger partnership and, thereby increase the chance of additional resource being available. Harry pressed Gillian to be clear what were her absolute fixed points and where was she willing to be adaptable. Harry felt he got some way with Gillian, but it was always going to be hard work. She was a reluctant coachee, but reached the point where she wanted to talk to Harry on a regular basis because she trusted his perspective on what was fixed and what was adaptable. Gillian thought Harry always asked brilliant questions which enabled her to differentiate in her own mind between what was fixed and what was variable.

In practice

- Encourage individuals to think through what are fixed points or variable factors

- Keep asking good questions to enable individuals and teams to come back to those principles

- Enable others to recognise the validity of fixed points and when it is folly to 'bash your head against a brick wall'

- Recognise that fixed points can change over time

- Enable others to see fixed points as important rather than as obstacles in the way

HAVING HONEST CONVERSATIONS ON PROGRESS

BELIEVING OUTCOMES ARE deliverable needs to sit alongside honest conversations about progress. Dreams can be helpful in sharing possibilities about the future. Delusions are ultimately destructive

The idea

Having clear aspirations means dreaming about what is possible. The vision about what is deliverable provides an incentive to see beyond the immediate and anticipate what is possible.

But every dream has to be tempered with realism. Every vision needs to be rooted in reality. When willing or reluctant partners work together, there needs to be honest conversations about progress. Some parties will have an interest in progress being seen more positively than reality. Others may bring a more cautionary approach and tend to see gloomy outcomes rather than signs of hope

Encouraging partners to be utterly objective about measuring progress and view it in a dispassionate way can bring an objective assessment which reduces the risk of an emotional reaction clouding subsequent actions. The advice from the leader as coach to be bold and to be honest about progress provides two important inter-connected perspectives. Encouraging both boldness and realism can lead to a reshaping of the dream or a revision of the timetable to deliver the ultimate aspiration.

Gillian in the operating theatre was utterly objective and calm. Outside the operating theatre she was passionate and could be over emotional. She could be inspirational one minute and talking about unrealistic dreams the next. Harry wanted to bring the best out of Gillian and help her channel her energy in the most productive way possible.

Sometimes Gillian would be over optimistic about what was possible and the progress being made. Harry was insistent in getting Gillian to be honest about progress on different schemes and the amount of backing she had for different ideas. Gillian was reluctant to listen but always knew that Harry would bring her back to reality and that out of those conversations would come some clear practical next steps.

In practice

- Face people up to the unreality of some of their dreams

- Ensure regular, honest conversations take place about progress

- Present honest conversations as leading to clear next steps

- Seek to ensure that honest conversations help focus energy and do not destroy it

- Be mindful about whether people are avoiding honest conversations

- Accept the short-term pain if others do not like your focus on honest conversations

65 DEALING EFFECTIVELY WITH DIFFERENCES

DEALING EFFECTIVELY WITH differences and conflict can strengthen the quality of shared endeavour going forward rather than erode it. Handling differences well unites rather than dissipates.

The idea

The leader as coach seeks to create a common purpose and build shared endeavour but the good leader will also highlight differences and use conversations about differences as a source of creative exploration. If there are two different perspectives there can be two constructive ways of seeing reality. Constructive dialogue about two different perspectives might well lead to defining a way forward that is more apposite than previous approaches. Out of difference can come new ideas and a crystallization of what a partnership is fundamentally seeking to do.

Discussion about differences can enable a better sifting of what is first order and what is secondary. The leader as coach encourages individuals and teams to put differences on the table and view them dispassionately. Effective dialogue is not about an aggressive or defensive exchange, it is about looking together at an issue and reflecting on the reasons for the differences. It can sometimes help to invite individuals to argue the opposite case to the position from which they started. Encouraging people to tell stories about how they have changed their mind and what has influenced that change of direction can create an openness to listen to each other and a greater willingness to move the thinking on.

To some, Harry and Gillian always appeared to be in conflict. They seemed to be talking about their differences much more often than their similarities. But the astute observer recognised that there was a mutual respect. They each wanted to hear the others' point of view. They each knew that their own thinking would be developed and sharpened as they listened to the other person. Because they had got to know each other well they could be frank with each other which could be unsettling for others.

Harry was quite right in emphasizing to Gillian that when they reached agreement on specific issues they needed to communicate the agreement that had reached and share some of the workings about how they got there. They wanted others to accept that the outcome was not a result of a battle of wits. It was an outcome which took account of different factors and was a result which the two of them were clear was a constructive conclusion.

In practice

- Ensure that differences are considered carefully and not brushed aside

- Encourage the exploration of difference as a constructive process leading to better outcomes

- Create a context where differences can be explored with passion and thoughtfully rather than emotively

- Encourage a clear articulation of how differences have been taken into account

- Do not encourage the belief that all differences can be removed as many have to be lived with

66 BUILDING ACCEPTANCE ABOUT THE NEED FOR CHANGE

Most people will be reluctant participants in change unless they accept the need for change.

The idea

We all have routines. Most organisations have patterns of activity. Most people prefer continuity to change. Perhaps five per cent of the population are 'change junkies', but most of us do not naturally rush to make changes.

As soon as we suggest to others that change is needed their first reaction can well be a defensive one with a reiteration of the benefits of the current status quo. Sometimes an individual will be articulating the benefits of the status quo, but at the same time recognising that all is not well with the current context and that some action is needed.

Building acceptance about the need for change may result from a crisis that surprises or unsettles people. The emotional hit that comes from a crisis can jolt people out of their current way of thinking and enable them to be more open to new ways of looking at a familiar issue.

Building an acceptance about the need for change may take time. It may need prompts and suggestions over an extended period. Inviting people to talk to others who have been through a similar process of change can build more of an acceptance about what is possible and a recognition that benefits can flow from change.

Inviting people to think, 'what would happen if we changed 'X'?' can be productive in inviting them to move into a different way of thinking about an issue so that they feel less constrained or inhibited in exploring some of the consequences, and potentially identifying some of the benefits.

John recognised that his team in Europe would need to become more efficient or some of its work would be transferred to India. The stark reality was clear to him but not so obvious to his team. The mindset of his team was that if they worked hard they would be appreciated and allowed to continue with their current work. Reality only began to hit home when some work from other teams was transferred to India. The reaction was one of righteous indignation and 'it will never happen to me'. John began to suggest quietly but firmly that the team needed to think about the implications of the company's policy to transfer more work to India and could not ignore the potential consequences.

John asked his team members to reflect on what might be the potential benefits. The team saw the consequences in other areas where work had been transferred to India of fewer jobs in Europe but the jobs that remained were particularly interesting. Those who had been part of this change in other areas talked of the excellent working relationships with colleagues in India and how progress came through using each other's strengths well. Eventually the team was ready to acquiesce in the transfer of some work to India while not being completely enthused about it.

In practice

- Be clear in flagging up the need for change
- Allow time for acceptance to develop

- Encourage people to talk through with others who have been through similar changes

- Do not be put off by the initial, emotional reaction of people, and recognise the grief that they are anticipating

- Be conscious about the signals you give in the way you respond to change and make the most of the opportunities that flow from the changes

67 CREATING A SHARED VISION ABOUT DESIRED OUTCOMES

ONCE A POINT of acceptance has been reached create time for a shared set of expectations to be put together.

The idea

In the early stages emotions can get in the way and mean that rational conversation is not possible. But once there is acquiescence that change is needed there is an opportunity to move through the pain barrier and encourage people to think through what the potential benefits might be. The line that, 'we may not want to be where we are, but how do we make the most of it?' can begin to prompt serious thought about what next. Once the reality of the situation begins to be accepted, putting some building blocks in place about what the new world might be like can become possible.

The line, 'what are our expectations about the difference we can make?' can change a spiral of despondency into an upward spiral working through possibilities. Turning the emotions so they look up rather than down begins to create a sense of possibility which dampens the sense of gloom. The more specific you can be about potential outcomes, the more the likelihood that they will be viewed as attainable, with it being worth putting in effort to reach those outcomes.

Once it became inevitable that some work would be transferred to India, John sought to build a clear understanding with his new senior colleague in India about the capabilities of their staff. They worked together on creating the right type of expectations about what work should be transferred, what the outcomes would be and how it would be delivered. John involved people in the UK and in India working together to define the precise nature of the work to be transferred and the quality standards that would be essential for its successful transfer.

John worked with his team on what would be their continuing work and the expectations about the quality of delivery of that work and how they would ensure that their customers thought that top quality work continued to be delivered, whether it was done in the UK or in India.

John was relentless in getting his people to focus on the quality of outcomes, and working together in a constructive way focusing on the delivery of those outcomes. Gradually the teams in India and the UK got to a point where they could talk about having a shared vision. John judged it would have been counter-productive to start at this point, but he thought he had reached a good outcome when staff in both countries wanted to develop a clear shared vision.

In practice

- Be specific about the desired outcomes and regularly repeat them
- Encourage the building of personal relationships between people who may initially be a bit frosty or uncertain, in order to get them to a point where they want to set out a shared vision
- Keep the focus on clear communication of those outcomes
- Face people up to the harsh reality if they do not work wholeheartedly towards those outcomes
- Allow doubts to be expressed thoughtfully in a way that informs and does not contaminate the enterprise

68 BUILDING CHAMPIONS

ALL CHANGE PROGRAMMES to be successful need champions at a range of levels whose judgement people trust.

The idea

The leader may be clear that change is needed but their words alone will not build acceptance or enthusiasm about change. The leader can set a sense of direction but they need others alongside them if there is going to be a momentum. Champions for change can be at any level within an organisation. Often the most effective champions are relatively junior staff whose practical views can affect attitudes across a whole organisation.

The best champions are volunteers rather than people pressed into service. When you are taking change through an organisation, keeping a careful eye out for those who might be champions is always well worth the effort. They may be champions because of self-interest or because they can see the longer term benefit. It might be that they have an insight into some of the opportunities that flow from the change. Whatever their reasons for supporting the change, legitimising their speaking out and encouraging others to listen to them can create a snowball effect. Just as a bad apple can affect a crate of apples, so an enthusiastic champion can enthuse across a whole organisation.

In the early stages of building acceptance about the transfer of work to India, John knew that if there were some champions then his task would be a lot easier. He encouraged a couple of people to visit India and get to know the people to whom the work would be transferred. When these two people returned they were positive about the quality of work that would continue to be done and the opportunity of joint working in other areas.

John invited some other members of his staff to think through what might be the opportunities to diversify some of the work they were doing in the UK and to explore how serious a prospect that was. They came up with some positive ideas about some new sectors, and a recognition that entering other spheres was unrealistic.

John encouraged these staff members to see themselves as ambassadors for the next phase. He encouraged them to talk to a wide cross-section of people and help build an understanding that there were potential benefits. The champions also had a role in helping people to recognise that change was inevitable and they could not keep going on as they were. The influence of these champions was both on people's thinking about next steps, and also on their emotional reaction to the prospect of change.

In practice

- Create opportunities for those who are curious to explore what the future might hold

- Allow people to develop their own thinking, and observe how their views on future possibilities evolve

- Build up the role of those who are influential and are positive about the future

- Bring together some of the champions so they can share their perspective and their belief in the opportunities

- Encourage people who are at very different levels in the organisation to become champions for change.

69 ENSURING A BALANCE BETWEEN REALISM AND OPTIMISM

ENABLING INDIVIDUALS TO hold a picture of the future which combines realism and optimism is crucial for success. With too much realism progress seems impossible. Too much optimism and it can feel that progress will be a myth and not substantive.

The idea

The long distance walker recognises the reality that it often rains in mountainous regions. Accepting reality means always carrying in the back-pack an anorak and over-trousers. But even when the rain is coming down hard the walker can look forward to the break in the rain and the sun bursting through.

The walker can always be optimistic that the sun will shine, while recognising that the sun might make its appearance on the following day rather than in the next 20 minutes. The walker keeps up their energy through the rain recognising that there will be a moment when the sun will shine and the rain will stop. This optimism keeps them going, even though they do not know when the weather will change.

When I co-authored a booklet, entitled, *Riding the Rapids* we talked about 'grounded optimism'. Leaders who had handled demanding times effectively talked of the need to be utterly realistic, but also to bring grounded optimism. What helped these people motivate their staff was this combination of bringing an attitude of mind that sees opportunities and is not ground down by harsh realities.

The phrase, 'every cloud has a silver lining' can sound trite but is often true. When individuals you are coaching are going through tough times asking the question, "might there be the silver lining to this cloud?" can enable people to reflect on what opportunities might be opened up or what constraints to past action might be less significant.

Members of John's team oscillated between deep gloom about the future and seeing possibilities for innovative work they could do with other colleagues in Europe and in India. John recognised that he needed to enable his team to feel grounded. In an away day he got them to focus hard on what they needed to leave behind in terms of the work they did and their attitudes. He got them to anticipate what might be a constructive outcome in the future and how best they could explore new opportunities.

John recognised that some people were moving more quickly than others to see opportunities. He encouraged those whose natural bent was to see opportunities to develop their ideas. John was relentless in bringing a grounded optimism about the future and knew that he must not dampen his resolve if he was to enable his team to be consistently positive about future opportunities.

In practice

- Be realistic in a way this is factual rather than just emotional
- Encourage others to 'look for the silver lining'
- Pace your energy so that realism does not look as if it is destroying your energy
- Bring examples from elsewhere in the organisation about how people have balanced realism and optimism effectively
- Describe the progress you see as part of the new reality

70 KEEPING BOTH FOCUS AND ADAPTABILITY

THE COMBINATION OF focus and adaptability is a characteristic of effective individuals and teams. The good leader is enabling individuals and teams to hold their nerve and evolve that balance.

The idea

My younger son played ultimate frisbee for Great Britain and has played for his club side, Clapham, extensively in Europe and North America. The good frisbee player is focused on where the frisbee is and where individual players are moving. The good frisbee player will have planned moves with their team but is able to adapt depending on the tactics of the opposition and the movements of his other team members. In any team game focus and adaptability are both crucial if the team is to be successful.

The team installing a new IT system has to be focused on the objective and able to deliver the milestones in a timely and consistent way. But the successful IT team has to be adaptable responding to the changing needs of the customer and to the problems of implementation. Holding to the original specification is important, but blindly following it can lead to disengagement and disenchantment from the customer if the customer's changing needs are ignored. Appearing to be too adaptable might lead to the focus being diluted on what is really important.

John knew he had to keep focusing on what opportunities might be possible going forward. His focus needed to be on creating a successful transfer of work to India while ensuring the day job was done, and keeping up a constructive perspective on the future opportunities. He had to recognise the changing energy levels of his people and respond to their identifying opportunities. He had to be mindful where energy was high and where energy was low.

John needed to adapt his approach and manner to ensure he was continually bringing out the best from his people in the day job, and in the thinking about the future. It was exhausting but rewarding too as he saw people adapt in a constructive way and talk positively where they had previously been downbeat.

In practice

- Be clear about your focus and ensure that there is consistency in the focus on what is important

- Keep emphasizing the balance between focus and adaptability and recognise when people are doing this well

- Create conversations where individuals are encouraged to think about what type of adaptability needs to be built in

- Be relentless about timetables to deliver focused outcomes

- Celebrate occasions when adaptability has worked well and led to a new, more pertinent focus

GROWING AN INDIVIDUAL WITH POTENTIAL

71 ENCOURAGE BELIEF IN WHAT IS POSSIBLE

AT THE HEART of growing an individual with potential is encouraging them to have belief in what is possible. This is not blind, pig-headed belief, it is belief based on competence, and hard work alongside realistic and bold aspirations.

The idea

Individuals can often either be too humble or too bold for their own good. Too humble and they do not realise their potential. Too self-important and others are content for them to fall or make a fool of themselves.

Letting someone have a realistic and bold set of aspirations can be a valuable way of enabling them to make the most of their potential. Practical approaches can include encouraging someone to:

- Reflect on what had been thought impossible before which had become possible

- Observe how others had turned supposedly impossible tasks into doable ventures based on taking one step at a time

- Crystallize what had helped them believe that something was possible in apparently unattractive circumstances

- Break a problem down into a series of steps so each step is seen to be attainable

Developing belief that something is possible allows both the rational and emotional parts of the brain to draw energy. It may take some time for an individual to think that a particular outcome is possible. Assertions from the boss that a task is doable will carry some weight, but does not bring overwhelming evidence. Often belief that something is possible only grows over time. An individual has to be given enough space and time for that belief to grow and then be affirmed and tested.

Jenny did not believe that it would be possible for her to give a good presentation to a senior group of stakeholders. She found lots of different reasons why it would not be right for her to take on this task. Her boss encouraged her to think of previous occasions where she had spoken well and to remember how she felt and what had given her energy. He encouraged her to believe that what had worked well with 20 people could work equally well with 80 people. Her boss allowed her time to reach her own views on how she was going to do further presentations. He gave her some practical tips and suggested that Jenny might rehearse the presentation with some colleagues. Her boss recognised that what he needed to do was to keep affirming quietly that she could and would make good presentations. The presentation went well and she felt she now had the confidence to speak at future events.

In practice

- Remember what had been achieved in similar circumstances before

- Recognise whether their usual perspective is to under-estimate or over-estimate what is possible and to be mindful of that going forward

- Break a daunting task down into doable steps

- Recognise what is going to sap or increase energy

- Enable someone to 'bank' progress and move on from this new base going forward

BRING FRANKNESS ABOUT NECESSARY DEVELOPMENT

REGULAR PRAISE IS important, but there must always be a clear appreciation of reality and clarity about necessary development.

The idea

We like to be able to praise someone and encourage them. It is a pleasure to see an individual be more confident and take on difficult tasks. We can be hesitant about giving too much advice about their development if we think it will act as a discouragement.

We want to treat people as adults and, therefore assume they know what is the right thing to do. We can think it is demeaning to draw attention to what further steps they might take. We do not want to be pernickety about what they might do next or how they might approach a particular issue. They are grown-up. It may be perfectly obvious to us what should be done next and, therefore, we think that another person will spot the 'correct' course of action immediately.

It might be worth reflecting on your own experience of when people have got the balance right in terms of being frank about your necessary development. The role models that you remember are likely to be people who did praise you and celebrate your success, but also pointed out at key moments how particular approaches had been interpreted and what might be worth considering as next steps.

Some of your memories might be about people who asked you good questions which enabled you to think through what was your necessary development. You may recall other people giving you more direct messages about what you needed to do to ensure success. How you remember those direct comments probably result from the quality of trust and respect you had with the individual giving the advice.

The way you enable someone to think about their necessary development will depend on your understanding of how messages are likely to be received and interpreted. For some individuals very specific advice about competences they need to develop is going to be what is needed. For others the encouragement is likely to be about entering particular types of situations without the need for any specific advice about how they handle those situations.

Where a relationship is working well your approach could be based on asking individuals to be clear what is the necessary development for them. It is about the setting up of a context where an individual can talk freely and ambitiously about their development. Your role may well be to affirm what they are saying and help create connections for them. You might also be adding a few thoughts or suggestions.

Jenny was not confident at chairing meetings. She tended to talk too much and not be well-structured. It was not entirely clear at the end of a meeting what the conclusions were and who was doing the follow up action. Her boss suggested that they might have a conversation about good chairing practice in which she encouraged Jenny to observe other chairs and reflect on what worked well or less well.

Jenny's boss invited her to identify three elements of good practice from people she observed chairing, and then encouraged her to reflect on which of those elements of good practice she was now going to adopt. Jenny put together some sensible action points with her boss only needing to do some gentle shaping, plus reminding her about the importance of clear summaries and action points at the end of items.

In practice

- Build on what is working well

- Be objective in your assessment about current reality and the need for development

- Be clear in your own mind what type of development is most important

- Seek as far as possible to enable the individual to reach their own decisions about their development

- Be willing to steer their conclusions where you think that one or two points are particularly important

73 CREATING STRETCHING SITUATIONS

ALL OF US need to be put into stretching situations if we are to grow. Creating or shaping the right type of stretching situations is crucial if individuals are to grow in confidence and competence.

The idea

When I was in the Combined Cadet Force at school I was useless on the assault course as I was incapable of climbing ropes. Repeated demands to try harder had no effect whatsoever as I could never get the hang of being able to climb a rope. But I relished the challenge of being given a difficult orientation task and being asked to get to a distant point in an efficient way. I hated and did not respond well to one type of stretching situation. I responded willingly and with alacrity to a different type of stretching situations.

We need to know our people well enough to understand what type of stretching situations will bring out the best in them and what will create apprehension, resistance or dejection. When we know what type of situations an individual relishes we can respond to their enthusiasm and enable them to 'stretch their wings' even more in stretching situations where they respond with both energy and resolution.

In stretching situations where we observe apprehension or even fear, our task is to enable an individual to work through those hesitations and understand what might work for them. Sometimes progress might come through approaching an issue from another angle, or agreeing initial steps that are modest and attainable without too much aggravation.

Sometimes deliberately asking someone to enter a situation which is going to be very stretching for them is exactly what is needed to ensure a step change in their confidence. If a junior member of staff has not been performing well you may want to put clear expectations on their boss about giving direct messages about performance and action that is needed. Building a plan about how this stretching situation is handled is a reasonable request for you to make of an individual prior to their having a difficult conversation with the junior member of staff.

Jenny knew that she had to raise the quality of work in one of her teams. Her boss saw Jenny as a shade reluctant to do this as some of the team were older than her. Her boss asked Jenny questions about how she was going to bring the best out of this team, and what did she want the results from the work of the team to be in six months' time. These clear questions challenged Jenny to think more explicitly about how she was going to manage this team to best effect.

Jenny recognised that she needed to be very clear about her expectations and talk with the team frankly about what was needed. Once she had been bold in setting out expectations and being frank about their limited success so far, two of the team rose to the challenge and did well. One member of the team left while another struggled. Jenny knew that her focus needed now to be on this latter individual where progress was slower but still there.

In practice

Recognise:

- Which types of stretching situations bring out the best in different people

- How you create a stretching situation which excites someone and brings out the best in them

- What type of questions you can ask which enable someone to stretch themselves and be realistic about what is possible

- How best you vary the speed of development you can expect depending on the experience, competence and mindset of the individual

- How you praise and encourage someone who is finding it difficult to handle a stretching situation

ENSURING CLEAR FEEDBACK

FEEDBACK MAY BE hard to take but is one of the most precious gifts we can give. Well-directed feedback can make a huge difference to an individual's performance and the fulfilment of their potential.

The idea

We often say we want feedback, and yet are reluctant to accept it and can be resistant to change. Feedback can produce a mix of emotional reactions in us that are not always predictable.

360° feedback is now much more common practice. Individuals are getting much more used to receiving feedback. Sometimes people become 'feedback junkies' and relish the receiving of feedback rather than putting the action and time in that is needed to address the key elements of feedback.

Feedback always says as much about the individual giving the feedback as it does about the recipient, hence the importance of encouraging someone to interpret feedback with care and not always regard it as golden words of wisdom. What matters is the pattern in feedback and how it reflects the nature of the relationship between the individuals giving and receiving feedback.

Just as important as ensuring that individuals receive clear feedback is setting the right context so that the feedback is heard in a constructive way. Using an experienced coach can make a difference in ensuring that feedback is used as a constructive basis for next steps rather than leading to diffidence and uncertainty that can undermine an individual's contribution.

When you want to give tough feedback to someone, how you do it is just as important as the messages you give. Creating the right context is important so that the giving of feedback is not rushed. Often a second conversation will be needed when an individual has reflected on the points you are making and has begun to work through their own next steps.

Avoid giving negative feedback right at the end of a conversation unless you can do so in a way which demonstrates your concern for the individual's well-being and success, and points to a subsequent conversation.

Jenny's boss knew that she had to talk to Jenny about her next steps in chairing meetings. There had been some progress, but Jenny was still talking too much in generalities in meetings, and was not being crisp enough in her summaries and next steps. Her boss flagged up with Jenny that it would be good to have a progress conversation about chairing of meetings and asked Jenny reflect on what she had experimented with.

Jenny began the discussion in confident vein talking about her perception of progress, but then recognised that there was further to go. Her boss talked deliberately and slowly about the feedback from some people that a further step-change was needed. Jenny recognised the points even though there was some frustration. The frustration was as much about herself as about others.

Jenny felt her boss had approached the issue well by flagging up the need for a conversation and giving her the opportunity to reflect on what progress she had made and what more was needed. Jenny knew it would take more time before she felt confident enough to get her interventions quite right. Following this conversation she felt affirmed in progress so far and clear about next steps.

In practice

Encourage someone to:

- See feedback as a gift

- Invite feedback and then look as if they welcome receiving it

- Recognise that the feedback will say as much about the giver of the feedback as the recipient

- Sift the comments and be clear about what specific points you want to take forward

- Recognise the best way of receiving and giving feedback

75 ENSURING CLEAR BUT NOT EXCESSIVE EXPECTATIONS

THE JOB OF a boss is to set clear expectations that are bold and realistic. They need to be stretching and doable. If they are excessive, energy will be sapped and not raised.

The idea

As a leader or manager you have a duty to set expectations that are clear. These are likely to cover the quantity and quality of what is done while giving an individual freedom about certain aspects of how they deliver those expectations.

The caring manager may not want to be explicit in their expectations but being too vague can create uncertainty with unnecessary energy being wasted as a result of a lack of clarity. An open discussion about what might be achieved by when can lead to expectations that drive action and stimulate energy. Those expectations need to be bold enough to create a sense of adventure and purpose, but doable enough to enable the confidence level to be high.

Sometimes it is right to set 'unreasonable expectations'. The leader whose people excel will have set the bar high. Where the leader is able to inspire their people they can set unreasonable expectations and individuals will respond and deliver what many had thought unattainable. But the leader who uses their motivational skills to get people to commit to seemingly unreasonable expectations must have a reasoned belief in their people and their capabilities. The inspiring leader will raise the sights of their people to climb the mountain. At the same time they will have checked the weather and ensured that they are not expecting their people to be fool-hardy walking straight into a devastating storm.

When an individual has been set clear expectations, a review conversation a few days later can help establish whether the individual has a plan which they are comfortable with, or, whether there continues to be an emotional reaction of exasperation and disbelief that progress is possible. Naming and talking through the emotional reactions can help remove some of the baggage which can get in the way of clear, unambiguous next steps.

Jenny felt that she had a lot of tasks to do and was not clear about expectations. She asked to talk to her boss so that she got a better sense of the boss's priorities. There was a mutual interest in setting clear expectations but her boss was honest that the uncertain position of the business meant that expectations could change rapidly. Jenny and her boss agreed on a set of expectations, but recognised that there would need to be flexibility. They scored some of the expectations in terms of how demanding they were and agreed when they would need to take stock together.

In practice

- Articulate your expectations and do not just keep them in your head

- Invite your people to play back to you what they see as your expectations, as their perception of what you want may be different to what you think you want

- Be realistic about what expectations are clear and fixed, and what are likely to evolve over time

- See the difference between 'unreasonable expectations' which are stretching but doable because they based on evidence about what is possible, and 'excessive expectations' which do not take proper account of what is doable

- Ensure that those who are to deliver the expectations can see a way forward and have the energy to deliver

MANAGING SOMEONE WITH LIMITATIONS

ENSURING AN OBJECTIVE PERSPECTIVE

WHEN YOU VIEW someone as having limitations it is important to ensure your perspective is objective and not contaminated by either your prejudices or those of others.

The idea

We all bring our own way of looking at individuals. We are conditioned by our upbringing, our education, our values and our previous experience. We may regard ourselves as entirely objective in the way we view other people, but we rarely are.

When we see someone as having limitations triangulating our view with others is important. There is a risk that people will tell you what they think you believe already. They may not want to disagree with the boss. There may be a competitive element which will mean that it is in the interests of the individual you are talking with to endorse your reservations.

How do you become as objective as possible in your assessment of an individual? What can help is to set some new tasks for an individual and review progress in a detached way right from the start. Setting clear milestones enables you to be clear on progress and to feedback to the individual your understanding of the progress made.

The discipline of writing down the expectations and the progress made is an important discipline to assist both the individual and you, and also provides an audit trail. The more you can get someone in a position where they are willing to write down their own assessment of progress and next steps the better. Sometimes agreeing and both signing a sheet recording agreed action can provide a benchmark against which progress can be measured. Sometimes it can be useful to involve a third party which can be another team member or a mentor or coach. Having a third party present creates a discipline and an independent memory about what has been agreed.

There is a balance to be struck between trusting your own judgement and asking questions about whether your own predilections are getting in the way. Talking your approach through with a trusted colleague can help give you an assurance that your perspective is accurate and strengthen your resolve about next steps.

Jeremy was conscious that George was not delivering the same level of performance as the other team members. George was not getting as many contracts agreed and did not seem as energetic as his colleagues. Jeremy wanted to look at the evidence from comparative figures over recent months before reaching a view on next steps.

Jeremy talked to a number of customers and a range of people within the organisation. It became clear that there was a pattern and that he needed to be frank with George about the evidence. He chose a natural review point, presented the evidence clearly and slowly giving George plenty of space to either agree or disagree. George set out a number of reasons for the problems, but accepted there was an issue that needed addressing.

In practice

- Collect factual evidence

- Triangulate your perspective with that of others

- Present the evidence openly to the individual

- Focus the discussion on the evidence and on next steps

- Try not to let your own emotions get in the way, while recognising the emotional reactions in the other person

77 UNDERSTANDING AN INDIVIDUAL'S CHARACTERISTICS AND EMOTIONS

THERE IS A risk that we think others will behave as we do. Understanding the world from their perspective is important if we are to improve their performance or enable them to move on with honour.

The idea

We are all unique. Everyone's brain is different. Our rational and emotional makeup comes from a wide range of sources and is continuing to evolve. Thankfully we are not clones of each other.

The use of personality profiles like Myers-Briggs has brought a much greater understanding about the preferences of different individuals. Understanding someone's preferences helps bring an insight into how best to convey messages to them so they receive messages in a way that is productive and not destructive.

Some people will absorb a message quickly and know how they are going to react to next steps. Others will need time to reflect and absorb before they will be ready to have a conversation about next steps.

Learning about an individual's family or cultural background can provide valuable insights into their values and personality. When we begin to understand the forces that have shaped someone we can more readily understand why they behave in the way they do. When an individual is reacting in a way which seems to us irrational, it is worth thinking yourself into their skin and trying to understand why they have reacted in the way they did.

Sometimes it can be helpful to note down what you observe about someone, what brings out the best in them and what brings out the worst in them. Understanding their characteristics can help explain why they act in particular ways and whether it is you who need to make the accommodation, or whether their approach is fundamentally flawed in terms of delivering what is needed.

As you understand someone's characteristics more, you may conclude that they have much to offer if the role is reshaped, or if they move to another part of the organisation. Or you may conclude that this is not the type of organisation which is going to bring out the best in them and it is time for them to move on.

Jeremy saw George's behaviour as inactive and too slow. He encouraged George to talk about his background which was from a rural community where time did not move quickly. The team had recently done a personality profile which showed George to be a reflector rather than an activist. Jeremy observed George needing a lot of reassurance when it came to making decisions and not wanting to rush them.

Jeremy recognised that he needed to demonstrate to George that he understood why he acted the way he did. He said to George that he recognised that George needed time to make decisions but encouraged him to set a timeframe by which he would make decisions and be active in taking forward his conclusions.

In practice

- Remind yourself of your own preferences and prejudices
- Observe others with a sense of interest and curiosity rather than disapproval

- Take time to build an understanding of the formative influences on someone's approach

- Pace conversations in a way that is compatible with an individual's characteristics

- Ensure that your message is direct and clear, while recognising how it will land, based on your understanding of the characteristics and preferences of the recipient of your message

78 HAVING AN HONEST CONVERSATION

YOUR EMOTIONS AND emotions of the other person may be getting in the way of ensuring clarity about next steps. What is important are honest conversations which are thoughtful, accurate, considerate and unambiguous.

The idea

We can get ourselves into the situation of feeling that if we are honest with somebody we are being unnecessarily cruel. But it is particularly cruel to someone to imply their performance is good and their prospects are bright when neither is true. Sometimes we have to be 'cruel to be kind'.

If someone's performance is not good and needs to improve, and if their prospects are not good there is a duty of fairness to be clear. We have a choice about how we present these concerns to an individual. We can present in a tone that sounds dismissive and unsupportive. We can also be honest in the assessment while recognising why it has happened and being constructive about what might be the next steps.

Creating the right context for an honest conversation is crucial. It needs to be in a private space with enough time for the individual to absorb what is being said. Feedback needs to be given in a way which allows for an emotional reaction and then time to work through to constructive next steps.

An honest conversation does not mean brutal, insensitive, abrupt feedback, but it does mean that the message is clear with the individual being asked to say what they have heard and what are the next steps that they are planning to take. Honesty in conversation is about openness based on clear evidence. It is about the performance of the individual and not an attack on their personal characteristics.

The more an honest conversation is based on evidence about current tasks, so it is depersonalised, the less threatening it is likely to be and the greater the prospect of a constructive outcome. When seeking to have an honest conversation with someone, it is right to ask yourself, are you being honest to yourself about the evidence and about the outcome you want to achieve? If it is time for someone to move on you may need to go outside your comfort zone and be frank and not wrap up your view in too many words.

Jeremy knew that the time had come to have a frank and open conversation with George. He waited for key evidence to be available on the contracts he was working on. Drawing from this evidence he said to George that they needed to have a conversation about next steps with a date for that conversation being agreed a few days in advance. Jeremy was open about the facts and asked George what he saw as the options. When George was reluctant to talk, Jeremy set out various possibilities about increasing the contract delivery level, or moving to another area of work, or potentially looking for a role in another organisation.

Jeremy put his concerns in a thoughtful and reflective way which George began to engage with. George opened up about some of the personal issues he was facing. It was clear that he wanted to stay in the organisation. George and Jeremy agreed some objectives going forward and agreed on the pattern of their forthcoming meetings. Jeremy was encouraged, but not convinced that significant progress would happen. Jeremy felt he had done the right thing in having an honest conversation and giving George another opportunity.

In practice

Be mindful of the importance of:

- Having honest, open conversations based on as much evidence as possible

- Creating the right type of space and timing for those conversations

- Giving forewarning that you want to have that type of conversation

- Creating an expectation among your staff that these type of conversations will happen

- Focusing on what needs to be done and how the individual is going to make progress rather than attacking the individual

- Ensuring there is agreement about next steps

79 BUILDING CLARITY ABOUT OPTIONS GOING FORWARD

THE MESSAGE 'TRY harder' is one we may want to give, but progress will be more likely if there is clarity about the options going forward and how best they can be achieved.

The idea

Inwardly you might be thinking, "if only this person pulled their socks up" and "tried harder", all would be well. Our emotional reaction is often that the individual could do better if a magic wand touched them on the shoulder and they became a 'better person'.

But shouting at the individual either physically or metaphorically works with only a small proportion of people. Progress is much more likely to come through building a practical understanding of why things are as they are and what are the next steps. When the long distance walker is lost, the message, 'try harder' is not what is needed. The walker needs to look around and pick out landmarks. They need to look at the map and the compass to orientate where they are. The walker needs to think through what pathways it might be appropriate to take in order to reach their destination. Or perhaps they need to retrace their steps back to where they left the path.

Building options with somebody going forward includes clarity about what needs to happen to become a good performer in the current role, and what the prospects are of a successful move to another role. The individual might also be encouraged to look at options externally, so they can use their experience in a different environment.

Jeremy was increasingly clear that George needed to think seriously about a range of options. When George's performance only increased marginally Jeremy said they needed to have a full discussion of future options. Jeremy was clear that he wanted to help George think them through options and provide whatever advice he could.

Jeremy encouraged George to look at his strengths and see how he might deploy them in a range of different roles. He encouraged George to think through what he would find most fulfilling if he were to stay in the current part of the organisation or move elsewhere or move outside. At this point George was not being required to reach a final conclusion but he knew that Jeremy was serious that the current situation could not continue as it was.

George recognised that he had to take the concerns of Jeremy seriously. For the first time he had to think about whether it might be better to move to another organisation. He looked again at his CV and updated it. He began to think into different roles in different organisations and identify what would give him satisfaction. He knew that he was not enjoying his current role and that recent results had been a wake-up call. It probably was right for him to move on although he did not intend to tell Jeremy this at the moment.

In practice

- There are often more options than you might initially think

- Pressing someone to think through different options may initially be an unwelcome wake-up call, but later be regarded as a constructive turning point

- Never be dismissive of someone as this will make your task and their task much harder in finding a constructive way forward

- Look for the spark that will enable someone to be energised to take on a new type of activity

- Believe that out of very difficult situations good can come both for the individual, you, and the wider organisation

80 MAKING HARD DECISIONS

A COACHING APPROACH does not remove the need for hard decisions. Sometimes a hard decision has to be made and implemented in a way that is decisive, clear, defensible and done in as compassionate a way as possible.

The idea

Bringing a coaching approach is designed to draw the best out of people. The aim is to enable the individual to think more clearly and act more decisively. But a coaching approach does not necessary lead to the right answer. Sometimes hard decisions need to be taken with finances cut, or structure changed, or products removed, or someone leaving the business.

Thinking through the implications of a decision must be right but continued procrastination leads to uncertainty and a loss of momentum and energy. The good leader spends quite a bit of time thinking about the timing of their decisions so that they are fully informed, but they do not wait too long.

The Crown Prosecutor needs to be collecting evidence, but if they leave a decision to prosecute for too long, witnesses will not be as readily available and the evidence may become less available.

Taking hard decisions well is about combining clarity about the evidence with an intuitive sense of what is the right thing to do that draws from your previous experience and your values. Often there is a moment when you need to have the courage to say, "this is what we are going to do" and link it with effective communication about why you are taking that action. When individuals are involved and there is pain and loss of income there will inevitably be emotions that might well hold you back from making a hard decision.

Using a coaching approach as a means of helping someone tackle an issue is an investment of your time and energy. When you feel that progress has been limited and you need to make a hard decision about someone's future, there is a risk that you might feel resentful. But investment in their development will never be wasted, even though it might not have produced the productive outcome necessary to ensure success in that particular role.

When a hard decision has been made and there has been a negative reaction to it, it is worth being clear with yourself about the reasons and the level of investment you put into the individual before reaching the point when a hard decision is needed. You can then 'hold your head up high' knowing that you had properly invested in the individual, and that you had been willing to make a hard decision when that became necessary.

As George continued to make limited progress Jeremy knew that he had to make a firm decision. Jeremy had an open conversation with George about the evidence being unequivocal that this was the wrong role for him to be in. They talked through a couple of different options about working elsewhere in the organisation or leaving. Jeremy said that he was willing to give George a couple of months before putting him on a performance regime. This gave George the opportunity to face reality.

George resigned before the two month period expired. He talked to trusted friends about his strengths and skills. He was going to take a break for a couple of months and then look for work in an interim management role. George did not like the conclusion that he needed to move on but thought that Jeremy had dealt with him fairly. He respected Jeremy's decision and was not resentful about it.

In practice

- You have a responsibility to make decisions having considered the evidence

- Making no decision is making a decision to let things drift

- Flagging up that you need to make a decision within a certain period can help you prepare emotionally to make that hard decision

- Talking through the evidence about why a decision needs to be made can help you prepare to make the decision

- It is always worth thinking through if some coaching conversations could help you work through a hard decision to move somebody on

SECTION K
BUILDING EFFECTIVE TEAMS

81 SEEING THE POTENTIAL

SEEING POTENTIAL INVOLVES looking ahead at what a team might be able to deliver and how members can draw the best out from each other.

The idea

You might have inherited a mixed group of people. It is rare that you have the opportunity to build a team from scratch but you may have the opportunity to make some appointments over time. The merits and demerits of your existing team will have been described to you by your predecessor and by others: you may be encouraged or apprehensive about what you have heard.

Your coaching of your team members starts from their current capabilities and reputation, but what might be their potential? What can you do to bring out the best in each member of your team? When you make appointments how can you ensure that those you appoint bring out the best in the current team members and develop their own contribution through interaction with existing team members?

When I work with a team I often ask them to reflect on the question, "What do I want from my colleagues which will bring the best out in me?" This often leads to a rich conversation with team members concluding that their colleagues are now more understanding of their approach and more committed to each other's success.

It can be helpful to reflect with each individual team member about the potential they want to draw out in themselves over the forthcoming months and the challenges they would like to grow through. An open and frank discussion about an individual's potential and how they want to develop will both strengthen the quality of your relationship and give impetus to their thinking about developing their own potential.

A conversation with a team which begins, 'what I can see us doing well in a year is', can produce a greater desire to work towards possibilities that had previously been ignored or dismissed.

Raj inherited a team of architects who had been doing fairly routine work over recent years. They had become unadventurous in what they bid for and in their designs. They stuck to methods that had worked well for them in the past, with the consequence that the team was regarded as dull and predictable. Raj knew that he had to set the team alight with more enthusiasm and more creativity. He needed to get them to believe they could experiment with new designs and be successful.

Raj arranged a team away day which began looked at a range of designs that other partnerships had produced. He stimulated members of the team to think about what might be possible and got them to imagine how they could work together in different and new ways. By the end of the workshop there was a new enthusiasm and a desire to experiment. They pitched for certain types of work which they had not bothered with in recent years: after some disappointments they began to be successful. Raj had enabled his team to believe that they had the potential to deliver innovative and up-to-date designs.

In practice

It is worth reminding yourself that:

- The reputation of the team may not describe accurately its potential

- Most teams want to be inspired and can, after prompting, see how they can become more effective

- Asking people to articulate what they need from their colleagues to bring the best out of them can be a powerful way of building openness and ambition

- Getting a team to articulate their potential can produce a description of success that defines what is worth aiming at

- Allowing a team to reach its full potential will mean your giving up some control to let the team grow

82 CREATE TIME FOR REFLECTION

Shared endeavour involves clarity of purpose combined with a strong sense of mutual support and a holding of each other to account.

The idea

Effective teams will have a clarity of purpose that is shared and which they can all articulate clearly and persuasively. If there is no clarity of purpose then the team members will be looking in different directions and taking satisfaction from different types of outcomes. A team might inherit a business plan, but it might not be a living document that members feel committed to.

Encouraging a team to stand back on a regular basis and reflect on what is its purpose may sound simplistic, but it can produce a revealing dialogue. Taking your team away for half a day reflecting on what is the purpose of the team and what success will look like in a year's time can lead to an insightful and stimulating exchange.

Greater clarity about the purpose of a team leads naturally into how does the team build a strong sense of shared endeavour? Building shared endeavour involves both an appreciation of each other's gifts and contribution, and an emotional bonding. The team leader as coach is trying to get to a point where all members of the team are committed to the success of the shared endeavour and to each other's success.

Building shared endeavour in a team includes building emotional connectivity, alongside a willingness to be frank about what is working well and less well. Creating opportunities where individuals affirm the value of each other's contribution, and have the freedom to make some development points can reinforce both hard-edged aspiration and practical support for each other.

Raj invited the architects in his group to work through how they could be mutually supportive of each other and share ideas and expertise more effectively.

They decided that every three weeks they would have a session when they shared ideas and when individuals would put forward some radical, initial proposals and seek views from colleagues.

Raj was clear that he needed to keep the energy moving upwards. He encouraged the architects to be more curious and be willing to adapt other people's ideas rather than stick to their previous approaches. He sought to build a culture where there was more mutual affirmation, together with more challenge about what was possible going forward.

In practice

- All human beings work better when they are emotional committed to their work

- Time out is never wasted looking at the purpose of a team and how shared endeavour can be built stronger

- An away half-day can help set a new direction, but the momentum needs to be maintained through effective review points

- Building shared endeavour always involves strong emotional commitment alongside honest, frank conversation

- Shared endeavour involves you as leader being consistently supportive and never dismissive of others' efforts

RECOGNISING CORPORATE LEADERSHIP RESPONSIBILITY

LEADERS HAVE A responsibility to deliver in their particular area and have a responsibility for the whole venture.

The idea

A leader or manager is going to be judged not only by the success of their area but also by the effectiveness of the whole organisation. It is too easy for an individual to gloat about success in their area, and ignore or be dismissive of what is happening elsewhere in the organisation. Individuals often ignore the reality that business success depends on the whole venture and not just how one part is contributing.

As leader of the team you want your people to be committed to success in their individual area and committed to the success of the overall venture. The way you describe your expectations will need to be clear so that people recognise that their performance assessment will include their contribution to the overall team and the leadership contribution role they bring across the whole organisation. Unless this expectation is explicit it may well be ignored or regarded as secondary.

You may ask individual members of the team to take on cross-cutting responsibilities either for particular projects, or for activities like training which can help build a sense of corporate leadership responsibility. But this approach needs to have teeth to carry conviction. You may want to say to an individual that they cannot receive a top performance marking unless they have contributed to the corporate leadership.

Practical ways of building corporate leadership responsibility might include asking members of the team to work in pairs on cross-cutting issues. Or, you might institute a practice of mutual mentoring, or deliberately ask a team member to review an area of work that is either in someone else's domain or is cross-cutting. Leading work on personal development, diversity or innovation across a whole team can provide an individual with wider insight, and build within them more of an emotional commitment to corporate responsibility.

Raj began to have conversations with his team about what was needed to ensure the team's success. Elements included professional updating, better project management, using each other's skills more effectively and ensuring there was good quality, professional challenge. Raj invited members of the team to take forward particular areas and then talk to their colleagues and produce a plan of action.

In management meetings the focus was much more on the success of the whole venture rather than progress in individual project areas. When Raj was away he asked different members of the team to take it in turn to be responsible for the team overall. This 'passing of the baton' helped create a stronger sense of team members having responsibility for the overall success of the team.

In practice

- Role-model effective corporate leadership so people see you as a leader of the whole organisation and not just your team

- Create formal, personal responsibilities which include corporate leadership responsibilities as well as accountability for delivery in their area

- Ask people to lead cross-cutting issues and recognise their contribution in doing so

- Move round the leadership responsibility for the team when you are away

- Be explicit when you think team members are not taking their corporate leadership responsibility seriously

84 ROLE MODELLING PARTNERSHIP WORKING

EFFECTIVE OUTCOMES OFTEN require good partnership working within an organisation and externally. Team members will mirror the way you model partnership working.

The idea

Team members will mirror what you do whether you like it or not. If you are aggressive they will tend to model that type of behaviour. If you are quietly persuasive there will be a tendency to use a similar approach with you and others. This tendency to mirror behaviour is an instinctive reaction. There will be occasions when individuals do the direct opposite, but more often than not the tendency is to follow the same style as the leader.

Therefore, if you want to build a strong partnership working among your team, the best way of encouraging this outcome is to model this type of behaviour with those you are building partnerships with. It is well worth thinking about who are the partners, you want to build relationships with both internally and externally and what might be the fruits of those partnerships. The more you can point to the outcomes that flow from those partnerships the greater the likelihood your team will want to adopt a similar approach.

Inviting team members to reflect on who they want to build partnerships with externally forces them to think beyond the boundaries of their immediate working environment and think through opportunities and possibilities. One approach might be a joint session with another team about shared projects, or shared ways of working, or pooling of expertise. Another approach might be to have a team discussion on partnership working and ask each member to talk through a couple of potential partnerships they want to build. Encouraging them to articulate benefits and next steps forces them to crystallize the actions they are going to take and enables the team to hold them to account about progress.

Raj was conscious that the architects often acted in their own silo. He wanted to ensure that a stronger sense of partnership was built up with the quantity surveyors and the engineers. He set up a joint session where there was a sharing of good practice on recent projects and an open discussion about how best the different professions could work together. It was agreed that they would develop a new way of working on two or three forthcoming projects using the professional expertise of the three professions to best effect.

Much of the work done by the architects was for a particular local authority. Raj was keen that a stronger sense of mutual partnership was built up with key people in the local authority. Raj talked to his opposite number about what would be the benefit of a stronger sense of partnership. Based on this agreement there was a short workshop based on drawing out examples of good practice and deciding on what would be the key ingredients of successful partnership working going forward.

In practice

- Live partnership working yourself and articulate its benefits

- Identify and praise examples of good partnership working

- Set up dialogues between different partners internally and externally

- Encourage others to talk through what are the potential benefits of different partnerships

- Hold people to account for the outcomes from different examples of partnership working

85 DRAWING OUT EACH OTHERS' CAPABILITIES

WE TEND TO take for granted each others' capabilities and don't always draw out those capabilities to best effect.

The idea

As leader of a team how do you bring out the best in the capabilities of each of your team, and enable them to bring out the best in each other? Sometimes this comes through direct comments to people suggesting that they use each others' skills and expertise in particular ways. Sometimes it involves deliberately asking people to work in pairs or threes on particular issues. On other occasions progress comes through inviting people to meet up with a remit to agree a couple of areas on which they are going to do joint work, without your specifying in advance what those areas are.

If you arrange a session with your team looking ahead at overall work priorities, it can be helpful to extend that to inviting team members to talk through what are their personal development priorities and how they want to develop their capabilities both as a professional and as a leader. Inviting team members to reflect on what is the value-added they bring now, and what is the value-added they want to bring in the future can help them crystallize the capabilities they want to grow. Then inviting the wider team to say how they would like to draw on these capabilities, can create a situation where team members are helping each other reinforce their own development and learning.

We often see other people with fairly blinkered eyes as we only observe their capabilities in a work context. It can be revealing to invite members of a team to talk about the capabilities they are using outside work, in the home, in the community or in a society, club or faith-based organisation.

Enabling someone to articulate what they have learnt about their capabilities organising a 'team' of children or a sports team can bring new insights about an individual's capability. There can be a flash of insight when someone talks about what they have contributed to the growth of the photography club. They may have shown skills in that setting or a greater confidence in that environment which can be translated across into a work context.

Raj was conscious that members of his team did not know a lot about each other and did not know necessarily how best to support each other. At the end of an away day they had an informal dinner together. He invited each member of the team to talk about what gave them energy outside the office and to share an experience of a group that they were part of. Examples shared included a choir, a cycling team, an extended family and a church: within each example the team member was playing an influential role. The team developed a much clearer insight about each other's wider capabilities which let them draw out the best from each other in a work context.

In practice

It can be helpful to encourage team members to:

- Describe what they are involved in outside the work environment and how that experience influences the way they lead at work

- Ask team members to share what are the capabilities they want to grow in forthcoming months

- Invite members of a team to suggest how they might support each other more fully

- Celebrate examples where two team members through working together have been able to develop each other's understanding and capabilities

BUILDING MOTIVATION IN AN ORGANISATION

RECOGNISING THE SIGNALLING EFFECT OF THE LEADER

THE LEADER'S DEMEANOUR, deeds and words have a much greater signalling effect than the leader often realises. Signalling what is important to you ripples right through your organisation.

The idea

You coach your people through your demeanour. If you look positive and walk around with a demeanour that looks engaged and purposeful you are setting a tone which other people will tend to follow. If you walk around looking as if you are carrying the cares of the world on your shoulders, others will feel the weight of the burden you are carrying. If your demeanour is one of accepting reality and yet viewing it in a way that is looking for opportunities going forward, then you will set a tone that others will want to follow.

People will read more into your demeanour than you intend. The first requirement of any leader as coach is to be mindful of the signals you are giving every day in the way you look. Even the way you dress is important. If what you wear is smart and measured, that gives a signal. If your tie is always undone and askew you are giving a signal whether you mean to or not. If you want to create a relaxed atmosphere, what you wear and how you move about is going to signal the atmosphere you want to create. The way you talk to people and the way you listen to their concerns signals what you believe is important. The way you prioritise your time will be scrutinized with individuals inevitably taking a view on whether you are using your time and energy well or not.

You do give some signals through your words too, but this comes third after your demeanour and your deeds. Words to be effective need to be part of short sentences including memorable phrases. Words and phrases that are important to you need to be repeated so messages are consistent. You may get bored with the repetition but allow yourself to believe that repetition is crucial, if clear messages are to be understood and remembered.

Maureen knew that she could be impatient and show impatience. She wondered why her staff was impatient with each other until someone pointed out the link between the two. Maureen recognised that if she wanted her people to exhibit a particular value then she had to live that value. She wanted people in her organisation to combine good listening with their making thought through decisions. She recognised that the best way of creating that outcome was to exhibit those characteristics herself. Her coaching task became easier when she was role-modelling patience, listening and decisiveness.

Maureen asked two or three people she trusted to observe her and give her feedback about whether she was living this approach or not. Maureen was conscious that there needed to be good examples of her combining patience, listening and decisiveness so that these stories went around the organisation and countered her reputation for impatience. She deliberately combined these attributes when making decisions on structure and funding, and articulated her own story about how she had combined these attributes. This helped build a greater appreciation about the value of combining patience, listening and decisiveness across her organisation.

In practice

- Be consistent in your demeanour, your actions and your words

- Be mindful of the signals you give every minute of the day from your demeanour

- Believe that your demeanour and deeds are coaching individuals all the time about what is good or acceptable behaviour

- Where your demeanour feels inappropriate take time out for five minutes to walk out of the building and then walk in again with the demeanour that you want to be living

- When you are signalling through words keep them simple and short and then repeat them

87 KNOWING HOW TO GENERATE ENERGY

WE CAN SAP or generate energy in others. The ability to generate energy in others is crucial to success in coaching.

The idea

Energy is not a finite commodity, it can go up or down. You as the leader can have a significant influence on the level of energy in others.

A starting point is being mindful about what generates energy in a team or in an individual. Asking members of the team to reflect on when their energy level is at its highest and what kills that energy, can be instructive. You have to be open to the response that you as leader can kill energy all too quickly. Asking individuals to reflect on what gives them energy or saps their energy can provide a very good barometer reading about what is working well or less well in your approach.

Helping an individual to work through what motivates them and how they can create energy in a situation which is new or difficult can help them unblock their approach to complicated issues. If we do not like doing something then we are less likely to be energetic in tackling it. A difficult issue will need more rather than less energy to handle: therefore, enabling an individual to reflect on what might give them energy in a tricky situation can help them find a means of building the momentum they need to tackle a difficult issue well.

Using a coaching approach is particularly valuable when working with someone on how they generate their energy as only the individual can judge what is going to sap or zap their energy level.

A directive approach will rarely work in enabling someone to garner their energy, the 'try harder' message is often going to be counter-productive and mean that an individual may exhaust themselves even more trying to obey that maxim in a potentially futile way.

Maureen was conscious that her audit team had to do a lot of audits in a short period of time. She knew that a message of 'try harder' would gain acquiescence but would not produce a lot of voluntary energy. Maureen talked with the team about how they would best handle this busy period and what would keep them energetic. Some talked about doughnuts and others about a drinks party when the audits had been completed.

Maureen asked them to reflect on what could she do to help. The response was about ensuring realistic timescales and minimizing the amount of additional work that was necessary at this busy period. Her people said that encouragement from her and recognition of work well done was important, as well as ensuring a supply of doughnuts on Fridays!

In practice

It is well worth being mindful of:

- The level of energy in a room and what raises it or lowers it

- Your own level of energy and why that goes up or down

- How best the energy of people in your organisation is maintained

- Recognising when energy runs low in others and how best it is raised

- Encouraging people to use energy levels as a barometer and be ready to switch activities to keep energy levels high

88 NURTURING CURIOSITY AND INNOVATION

Nurturing curiosity and innovation is crucial in order to keep teams and individuals fresh and alert and ready to try new approaches.

The idea

Curiosity might have 'killed the cat' but without curiosity we stagnate. A starting point for nurturing curiosity and innovation in others is to be continually curious yourself. If your mindset at the start of each week can be, 'what am I going to be curious about this week?', then you are more likely to spot opportunities that you want to explore.

When our children were young we used to suggest that we look out for red cars. We then discovered that there were many red cars. When we switched to blue cars we discovered that there were many blue cars as well. If we look for different ways of tackling situations and innovative approaches we are much more likely to see them.

Members of a team will have a natural inclination to focus on their jobs and to deliver what is expected of them. If we ask them to be curious about the wider world they may think we are distracting them. But if we encourage them to observe how others are doing similar tasks and what can be learnt from observation, they are more likely to see curiosity as a constructive exercise and not a distraction.

Coaching others is about inviting them to be curious and suggesting they talk to people in different parts of the organisation, or in different organisations or parallel worlds. The more you can encourage someone to have the mindset of looking for ideas that are working elsewhere that can be transferred, the more curiosity will become an accepted and cherished behaviour.

This is not about advocating innovation for the sake of it, but it is about identifying good practice and then seeking ways in which that good practice can be translated into your organisation. Good coaching is about stimulating others to want to innovate and grow ideas, and then giving them the support to implement those ideas.

Maureen knew that some of her auditors were set in their ways. They followed good, professional practice but sometimes in a way that was rigid. Maureen built a link with another auditing organisation. Staff from the two organisations met and had some shared training. There was a curiosity about how others did similar tasks.

Lively discussion led to some of Maureen's auditors being much more enthusiastic than she had expected about the joint conversations. She detected that many of the auditors were now more open to new ideas and more willing to innovate. She felt that a corner had been turned. She built on this greater openness by inviting in some experts who helped build stronger capabilities in some of her auditors in new fields.

In practice

- Be curious yourself and tell stories about how you have followed your curiosity

- Legitimise others being curious and sharing their stories

- Enable your people to meet with others in parallel organisations to talk about innovation

- Publicly recognise examples of good practice and forward innovation

- Encourage conversation in small groups about what type of innovation needs to be taken further forward, and why

BUILDING HOPE AND EXPECTATION ABOUT POSSIBILITIES

WITHOUT HOPE WE die. If there is expectation about possibilities we are much more likely to be motivated.

The idea

When times are tough being able to point to 'light at the end of the tunnel' can keep people going. The phrase, 'there is a silver lining to every cloud' can be a useful piece of self-talk for every leader. Every difficult situation creates some benefits even if it is just a reminder of what is important, or a development of personal resilience, or evidence of an individual growing into being able to take on more responsibility well.

Building hope is based on an accurate assessment of current reality, and then an openness to what might be the opportunities going forward. Every harsh reality creates new opportunities, even if it is just an acceptance that tasks can be done in different ways and that a new sense of priority can flow from seemingly devastating situations.

A key role for the leader as coach is to encourage people to be clear about the realities of their situation and to look for opportunities. The question, 'what does this situation open up as a new way forward?' can be a powerful open question. The leader as coach is giving people time to reflect and not asking for immediate answers. The encouragement to 'look up to see if you can see the light at the end of the tunnel can help create a mindset of looking for the good rather than being devastated by the bad.

Where funding is tight any group has to think about new ways of doing their job well. The leader as coach will be creating opportunities to think radically about what tasks can be done more simply, or what can be dropped altogether. The continued revolution in IT provides new ways of processing and passing information. Encouraging your people to leave behind previous ways of doing things and keeping searching out new ways is a never-ending process.

Maureen's auditors were beginning to protest that they should not have less resource even though the rest of the organisation was receiving less funding. Maureen set up some workshops where the auditors shared good practice and worked on how they might reduce the time spent on some audits and produce simpler and clearer reports. There was a fear that this might mean certain corners were cut, but there was also a recognition that their reputation depended on being responsive and efficient with their audit reports being readily interpreted and easily applied.

Maureen talked with the auditors about the possibility of extending their work into other organisations but emphasized that this depended on their continued efficiency and effectiveness. Maureen sought to build high expectations amongst her auditors alongside a willingness to be increasingly efficient in the way they operated.

In practice

- Link realism and the search for new openings together

- Use stories about how new openings have come out of tough experiences

- Encourage people to see possibilities in every situation and always to be looking for the light at the end of the tunnel

- Allow yourself to be excited about future possibilities and let that show

- Highlight those people who are focused on new opportunities and encourage them forward in a positive way

90 ENSURING CONSISTENT BEHAVIOUR

THE CONSISTENT LIVING of behaviours and values in an organisation gives people the security to be able to respond in a consistent way which builds mutual respect and trust.

The idea

Any organisation needs a good level of mutual respect and trust for it to work smoothly. Where trust is thin people are 'watching their backs' and cautious about what they say and do. If they feel they are going to be briefed against or criticised behind their back they will be cautious and reluctant to push forward new approaches.

When behaviours in an organisation are inconsistent far too much energy will be wasted watching others and in internal politics. Where a set of clear values or behaviours have been developed and are known within an organisation, then there is a touchstone against which the attitudes of individuals can be measured. When there is a pattern of consistent behaviour there is a much greater likelihood that individuals will feel relaxed in the way they work within an organisation and able to contribute fully.

Inappropriate behaviour needs to be identified with action taken. Where there is bullying or anger there needs to be a track record that such behaviours have been addressed and not repeated.

The leader as coach needs to be living a set of clear behaviours and endorsing positive and consistent behaviours so that the individuals can be secure in knowing what is acceptable or unacceptable behaviour and thereby willing to operate within that framework.

People are much more likely to flourish in an organisation whe...
consistently good behaviour is recognised and endorsed.

Maureen was conscious that some of her auditors had a reputation
for being rude to customers. There was a risk that they hid behind
their professional role as auditors and had got away with being
abrasive for too long. Maureen was clear that this attitude needed
to change to ensure that the relationship with client organisations
was more constructive. She organised a workshop on effective
influencing skills with clients which endorsed a set of principles
about effective behaviour. She then put a clear expectation on her
team leaders to keep an eye on whether those principles were being
followed and to talk individually to anyone who was demonstrating
abrupt and dismissive behaviour.

In practice

- Demonstrate consistent behaviour yourself

- Seek means of building trust between members of your
  organisation and external partners

- Be clear what type of behaviours are not acceptable and
  demonstrate that you have tackled instances directly

- Never shy away from tackling inappropriate behaviour

- Be ready to forgive if there is clear evidence that an individual is
  going to behave consistently going forward

DEVELOPING RESILIENCE
AND ADAPTABILITY

UNDERSTANDING THE EFFECTS OF THE INDIVIDUAL'S RECENT HISTORY

THERE IS ALWAYS an explanation for someone's approach or behaviour. Knowing about their recent history can bring helpful insights.

The idea

We are all captive to recent events in our lives. Our minds can be distracted by financial and practical concerns at home. Our emotions can be overlaid by reactions to sad or joyful events. We are always a rag-bag of emotions whether we care to admit it or not.

Understanding someone's recent history can provide indications about their level of resilience and adaptability. The pain of bereavement or broken relationships may be obvious and flow through into an emotional brittleness. But sometimes the emotions are more hidden where there is frustration with an individual or unrealised ambition, or a sense of failure about individual projects not working well.

Asking open-ended questions about what is happening in an individual's life is not prying or rude. The individual has the choice whether to answer the questions. A reasonable quality of relationship needs to have been built up first before it is appropriate to ask questions of a personal nature. But if you are able to create a context where people share what is frustrating them or engaging them outside work, it does give you an understanding of their level of resilience and what might be affecting their adaptability.

This information can enable you to make allowances for an individual's circumstances, without doing it in a way which is then unfair on other members of the team who might become resentful if they feel they are carrying an extra burden unreasonably.

Bob was conscious that Colin sounded more edgy that usual. Colin was not thinking issues through before making decisions. He was as conscientious as ever but did not always seem fully focused. Bob asked open-ended questions about what Colin had been doing at the weekend and got vague responses. Bob decided to leave this subject but continue to observe Colin's approach.

Bob had conversations with Colin about a couple of pieces of work that were not up to his normal standard and asked an open-ended question about why these pieces of work had not been as thorough as in the past. Colin began to talk about the illness of one of his children. Bob understood more what was happening in Colin's life.

The consequence was that they agreed a revised timescale for two of the pieces of work Colin was doing and agreed that the standard of the work needed to be maintained. Bob was glad he had opened up the subject and had given Colin time and space to think through how much he wanted to say.

In practice

Be mindful of:

- Unexpected patterns in the behaviour of individuals
- When to ask open-ended questions to seek understanding

- The importance of creating space for confidential conversations without putting pressure on anyone

- The need to adapt your requirements on an individual while continuing to be fair to others

- The importance of continuing to believe in an individual's capabilities and not allowing a temporary dip in performance to unnecessarily change that perspective

92 KNOWING THE EMOTIONAL PRESSURE POINTS

Each individual and team has emotional pressure points. Recognising what they are and choosing the moment to address them, or work around them, is important to enable someone to progress

The idea

Each of us has emotional pressure points when we become annoyed, angry, frustrated, disengaged or stressed. We may have learnt how to handle these emotional pressure points and have trained ourselves to recognise the early warning and then to avoid the more acute of these reactions.

In an open, working relationship the boss should be able to ask individuals what are their emotional pressure points, how do they anticipate them and then handle them. This is not an invitation for someone to download all their emotional problems, but it is about inviting them to recognise what are the emotional pressure points in the work situation that can get in the way and create reactions that can be damaging or counter-productive.

Sometimes an appropriate way to address an emotional reaction is to invite discussion about that response a few days later. It is rarely right to do it immediately as the emotional reaction might be overwhelming and mean the discussion is not as thoughtful as it could be. The risk is that the conversation never happens, hence the value of inviting a conversation a few days after an emotional reaction with a view to understand what had happened and why. This can encourage an individual to think through how best to handle a similar situation the next time round.

Colin was normally a good participant in meetings who listened well and contributed thoughtfully. But on a couple of occasions Colin had been short and abrupt with a colleague. When it happened a third time Bob decided that he ought to raise it with Colin. At the end of a meeting a couple of days later Bob asked Colin if he would be content if they reflected on Colin's contribution in some recent meetings.

Bob praised Colin for his valuable contributions giving some examples of his impact. He then raised the interaction with the other colleague and asked why Colin had reacted to him in the way he did. Initially Colin looked hurt but then recognised the concern and explained that the colleague had been abrupt with him on other occasions.

Colin volunteered that his response was churlish and acknowledged that his reaction was inappropriate. Colin was more circumspect in the way he responded to the colleague in future. Bob was pleased that he had raised this question in a gentle, open-ended way.

In practice

- Acknowledge that we are all human and have emotional pressure points

- Invite people to talk about their emotional pressure points and how they handle them

- Use open-ended questions to allow someone to reflect on how they have responded to emotional pressures

- See emotional reactions as often a good thing demonstrating passion and commitment

- Encourage someone to observe their emotional reactions in order not to be captive to them

93 GROWING PERSONAL RESILIENCE

ENABLING SOMEONE TO grow their personal resilience is perhaps the most significant contribution a manager can make to enabling an individual to progress

The idea

It is worth enabling your team members to reflect on the sources of personal resilience that come from their background, their physical and emotional make-up, their values and beliefs, and their family and their friendships. The more an individual understands their sources of personal resilience, the better equipped they are to understand others and enable their staff to develop their own sources of personal resilience.

Personal resilience comes from different sources. Knowing someone's parental and cultural background can help give an insight into the nature of their resilience. Once a working relationship has been established it is a reasonable question to ask someone about their sources of personal resilience.

If you are planning an away half-day for your team, part of the discussion could be about sources of personal resilience. It can be revealing to ask people to share what enables them to be resilient and how they want to continue to build that resilience.

As a team looks ahead posing the question, "what will help us be resilient as a team going forward?" can be a good way of drawing out sensitivities and creating mutual understanding. A team reflecting on how they have been resilient in the past and what they learn from that experience can be valuable in enabling members of the team to be more confident in each other.

Bob recognised that Colin had shown signs of fragility in some situations where he had felt criticised by others. Bob used one of his one-to-one conversations with Colin to invite him to reflect on what are the sources of his resilience and what was continuing to strengthen that resilience. Colin talked about his commitment to the work and a growing sense of passion that he could make a difference through his contribution.

Colin said that the knowledge that he had influenced key projects and helped ensure successful outcomes was enabling him to build his internal resilience and be less thrown by criticism from others. He was learning to interpret the criticism as about the work and not about himself.

De-personalizing the criticism was helping him treat it more objectively and respond to it in a more constructive way. Colin felt he had a good level of physical resilience but needed to keep building his emotional resilience. He recognised that it was sometimes three steps forward and two steps back, but began to see how he could make progress..

In practice

- Share your own stories about building personal resilience

- Encourage someone to identify what are the sources of personal resilience that have worked well for them in the past

- Enable someone to assess how their level of personal resilience has changed

- Encourage an individual to be explicit about what they need to do to build their personal resilience

- Create a context whereby members of a team can share their own stories about their intentions for building personal resilience

94 DEVELOPING AGILITY AND APTABILITY

ENABLING INDIVIDUALS AND teams to be agile and adaptable is essential in a fast-changing environment

The idea

Agility is about the mental and emotional approach and is not just about physical fitness. Inviting individuals and teams to reflect on what are the characteristics of agile individuals and teams can provide a rich source of insight. The agile cyclist is bringing physical excellence alongside mental determination and the emotional ability to handle a wide range of different situations. The successful cyclist is operating as an individual and as a member of a team when joining in a peloton and taking turns as leader and follower.

Inviting an individual to reflect on when they have been at their most agile and what they have learnt from that experience can provide lots of practical examples that can be built on. Inviting a team to think about when they have been at their most agile and what they learn from that experience can be an effective way of enabling a team to take stock.

Agility is about the focused use of energy, bringing foresight, being mindful of what others are doing and choosing the moment to take the lead. The successful, agile sports person is a good follower and a good leader. They can vary the pace and know what is needed to do well in an overall event.

Encouraging someone to be adaptable is about helping them crystallize the range of the repertoire they bring and how best to use different parts of their repertoire. The agile athlete is not always predictable. The adaptable leader will be varying their approach in a deliberate way responding to the needs of different situations.

Colin ran half-marathons. Bob encouraged him to reflect on what he learnt from doing half-marathons that was relevant to his work. Colin talked about the training and the pacing of the runs. He described having a clear picture in his mind of the finishing line and how he mentally celebrated reaching certain milestones. Colin was animated in describing the training and what works for him.

Colin began to see how some of his techniques in training might apply to his work, particularly in having a clear vision about where he wanted to get to and celebrating milestones on the way. He began to joke about seeing different projects he was involved in as akin to a forthcoming half-marathon. Reflecting this way brought a lightness to the way Colin described some of the next steps in his work. The consequence was that he took certain difficult meetings less seriously and got less bogged down and dejected.

In practice

- Encourage individuals to reflect on their own agility and how they use it
- Draw parallels from sporting activities that individuals or teams observe or engage in
- Enable people to reflect on the balance between core strength and agility
- See the willingness to be adaptable as a strength and not a liability
- Encourage individuals to reflect on what are their next steps in becoming more agile

95 KEEPING FIT IN BODY, MIND AND SPIRIT

KEEPING FIT INVOLVES both activity and rest. Wellbeing flows from keeping fit in a variety of aspects of life..

The idea

Keeping fit is not all about activity. It is about balancing activity and rest. Fitness involves understanding your body and how best you keep your body, mind and spirit fresh and alert.

The good leader is observing the wellbeing of their team members. They are conscious that there is an interaction between physical, mental, emotional and spiritual wellbeing. The good manager is not imposing any particular view, and yet carries a responsibility for the wellbeing of their people. The good manager may well want to be encouraging as individuals talk about how they keep themselves physically fit. They might encourage individuals to talk about what aspects of life outside the office give them energy and purpose.

The good manager might encourage someone to keep a wide perspective in their reading or in their observation of others and continually be developing their understanding of people and situations. Without imposing any particular view the good manager may be using opportunities to invite an individual to reflect on the relationship between what matters to them overall in life and what they want to contribute in their work.

When an individual begins to look bored or disengaged the manager has a responsibility to ask questions and help stimulate fresh thinking and help raise the level of motivation if it looks to be flagging. Asking an individual in the latter part of a performance review discussion about what will enable them to keep fit and fresh in their body, mind and spirit is not an unreasonable question. Each manager has a duty of care for their people.

Bob knew that Colin was finding his sports training difficult. He had stretched a muscle which had limited his suppleness. This restriction on his physical fitness meant that his enthusiasm at work was dulled and there was a flatness in his approach. Bob invited Colin to reflect on what was the link between his physical, mental, emotional, and spiritual wellbeing. This open-ended question legitimised Colin's thinking through and articulating what was the relationship between these different strands.

Colin used his gradual return to full training to introduce a discipline into what he was reading outside work. Colin knew that he would benefit from a wider stimulus reading articles about the effect of new technology on social attitudes. Colin knew he needed to keep fresh emotionally, mentally and physically and was glad of the prompting from Bob to look at his overall wellbeing.

In practice

It is worth encouraging individuals to:

- Reflect on their level of physical fitness and how they are going to enhance it

- See the links between physical, emotional, mental and spiritual wellbeing

- See time spent investing in their own wellbeing as a valuable, long-term investment

- Be open to different ways of maintaining their wellbeing

- See the parallels between keeping fresh in one area of life and applying that approach to keeping fresh in other areas of life

SECTION N
ENABLING AN OPENNESS TO CHANGE

96 SEEING LIFE AS AN EXPLORATION

THE MORE LIFE is seen as a journey of exploration the more alert individuals are to their environment and to opportunities.

The idea

I recently did a long distance walk in north west England called the Ribble Way. I lost the route and wanted to do a short-cut to get back onto the route. I saw a damp piece of ground which I thought I could easily cross, but I found myself sucked down into a bog up to my thighs. I was stuck and wondered if I could get out. I scooped up the mud around my right thigh and eventually squelched my leg free. I then did the same with my left foot and finally crawled across the bog to safety. I had to cope with the unexpected on what should have been a fairly routine walking day. I have subsequently used this experience as a metaphor about life as an exploration and coping with the unexpected.

Enabling people you coach and mentor to see life as an exploration with unexpected surprises is part of the joy of coaching work. As you draw examples from your own journey you can help individuals prepare for the unexpected and keep up a curiosity and sense of adventure which will enable them to maintain their energy and curiosity, even when they feel as if they are stuck in a bog.

Helen thought long and hard about how she could bring the best out of Sandra as a newly promoted organisational development consultant. Sandra was relatively set in her ways, liked routine and was fairly predictable in her approach. Helen could see the potential in Sandra and asked Sandra what brought out her sense of adventure.

Sandra began to reflect on her enjoyment of riding a bicycle in the country and going down different lanes without knowing precisely where the lane would end up.

Helen began to encourage Sandra to do more cycling if that gave her joy. Helen began to reflect with Sandra on what she enjoyed about this exploration into the unknown and how that might be transferred across into a work situation. Sandra talked about being prepared and having the right equipment and then being willing to be adaptable as the lanes went up and down. Helen enabled Sandra to talk about the sense of fun she got from cycling and how that sense of fun might be replicated in an office situation.

In practice

See opportunities to:

- Describe your own sense of exploration and what you learnt from it

- Encourage others to talk through what they had explored and learnt from that exploration

- Enable others to reflect on when they got 'stuck in a bog' and how they got out of that situation

- Encourage others to see twists and turns as adding to the interest rather than being distractions

- Recognise how people respond in very different ways to a twist in the road

KEEPING THE BALANCE BETWEEN FIXED POINTS AND NEW INSIGHTS

ENABLING SOMEONE TO find the right balance between what is fixed and unchangeable, alongside new insights and ways of addressing issues is essential to an individual's equilibrium and success.

The idea

The individual who is successful knows what the fixed points are and what they cannot change. They put their focus on what can be changed and where new opportunities exist. There are moments when a leader needs to change everything at the same time. But more often than not the successful individual will recognise what are the constraints that need to be respected alongside the openings that are there to be taken advantage of.

There is no point in encouraging someone to 'bash their head against a brick wall' when there are immoveable obstacles to change. Good coaching is all about encouraging someone to see where there might be opportunities, and to be alert to when is the right moment to press a point.

The leader as coach emphasizes timing as much as content. At one moment someone's idea might be regarded as an irrelevant distraction. A little later it may be a brilliant insight. There will be times when the individual has to accept not being heard: the individual who wants to bring new insights needs to be prepared to be patient and then opportunistic in putting them on the table.

Part of a forward-looking one-to-one conversation can be to encourage someone to talk through the balance between fixed points and new insights they want to bring, so that they are ready to take an opportunity and are prepared emotionally to do that and not feel rebuffed on the first occasion.

Sandra was thinking through how to persuade the hospital management to look at a new way of managing the porter staff. Sandra feared that the first time she suggested changes to the arrangements she would be criticised as being a consultant who did not understand their issues. Helen encouraged Sandra to talk through with the key managers at the hospital what was the problem they wanted to solve and what difference it would make if the problem was solved. Her advice to Sandra was to build a strong sense of rapport and shared interest in solving this problem.

Helen encouraged Sandra to have a number of possible ideas to suggest and see which began to land. She suggested that Sandra demonstrate her flexibility in shaping these ideas enabling the managers to make the decisions based on thought through options. Helen encouraged Sandra to think of the interchange as a friendly, relaxed dialogue which would encourage the manager to look in an open minded way at the possibilities.

In practice

- Be open about your approach to balancing fixed points and new insights

- Encourage someone to test out the reasons for fixed points and to reflect on the degree of flexibility that is possible

- Enable someone to see the timing dimension as important without feeling the need to rush into solutions

- Create a sense of lightness in conversations about fixed points and fresh ways of doing things

- Recognise there is always a reason for apparent fixed points, even though you might want to encourage someone to shift their perspective

98 ALLOWING LEARNING TO BE NEVER ENDING

THE ENCOURAGEMENT TO see learning as continuous creates an openness to new ideas and changing attitudes which is essential for any successful manager.

The idea

If someone thinks they have nothing to learn they become blind to what is happening around them and close off new understanding and insights. The speed of change in both technology, financial availability and attitudes means that anybody who is going to make their mark in an organisation is going to have to be continually learning.

The good manager is describing on a regular basis what they have learnt and how they have turned that learning into practice. They are praising the learning that they observe in others and creating the right contexts for people to share their experiences and learn from each other.

As a coach I encourage the people I work with to reflect, at the end of each project, and in each month of their lives, on what they have learnt. The question, "what have your learnt this month?" may seem boring to repeat but can be profound in encouraging individuals to keep crystallizing what has been their learning and what are their next actions.

The good leader of a team is inviting the team to take stock regularly about what they have learnt about effective leadership and about effective dialogue between members of the team. The good team is learning how to cope with the unexpected and with conflict, and the best way of taking forward new opportunities.

Helen sometimes felt irritated by Sandra because of her apparent reluctance to be open to new learning. Helen knew that she should not let this irritation get the better of her. Helen decided the right approach was to talk in a positive way about what she herself had been learning from a recent course and as a consequence of working with her coach. She thought that this might be infectious.

Helen asked Sandra what she was hoping to learn over the next few weeks. When Sandra gave a non-committal response Helen, with a smile on her face said, "what might you like to learn over the next few weeks?!" This teasing approach led to comments about talking to colleagues in another team about approaches they had been developing. Helen followed this interest and suggested that a dialogue might be set up to exchange ideas with members of that team. Sandra responded positively to this and Helen made sure the dialogue happened within the next few weeks

In practice

- Keep sharing your own learning

- Bring out the excitement of new learning

- Create situations where colleagues can share what they have been learning and how it can be applied

- Create time where individuals can do short courses or workshops or receive coaching and mentoring

- Encourage individuals to summarize on a regular basis what they are learning

99 BELIEVING THE IMPOSSIBLE IS POSSIBLE

Effective change only happens when people believe that what is described by some as the impossible is possible

The idea

When there is an inner belief or assumption that an outcome is not possible, that outcome will never happen. The role of a manager is often to unbolt in someone an existing assumption that an outcome is not possible. If the bolt can be unlocked and there can be light coming round the edge of the door then belief is opened up that change is possible.

If someone is downcast thinking that an outcome they want to achieve is not possible, a fruitful conversation can be about when have you felt this way before and the outcome has been delivered. Often there are repeat patterns in negative attitudes and behaviours that limit the appreciation about what could be possible going forward.

The question, "is there a self-limiting belief that is getting in the way of progress?" can be a slightly provocative question that can help unlock the bolt. Sometimes an assertion that something is not possible will be an accurate reflection of reality, with it being folly to believe that there can be any progress at this time.

Enabling someone to break down a project into steps can turn the seemingly impossible into a perfectly possible sequence of steps. What had previously been felt to be unattainable then becomes within the realm of the possible. The risk to avoid is assuming that once the first step has been completed, the end result will be easy.

The belief that the outcome is possible one step at a time does mean one step at a time.

Sandra thought it would be impossible to persuade the client that they needed to change the structure of their organisation. Helen coached Sandra by inviting her to reflect on how she had helped similar individuals to move on in their thinking. Who might Sandra introduce her interlocutor to who would share some parallel experiences? How might Sandra describe the steps needed to reach a radical outcome in a way that enabled the steps to look attainable and reasonably attractive?

When her interlocutor agreed to visit a couple of other hospitals Sandra knew there was a chink of light. Following these discussions the door began to open 'of its own accord'. What was previously off the agenda was now was not being described as a possible and attractive way forward.

In practice

- Share stories about how the impossible had become possible

- Use visual pictures like locked gates that can be unlocked

- Encourage action to be considered as a sequence of short steps

- Create opportunities for people to talk with others about how they have turned the impossible into the possible

- Look encouraged when someone talks enthusiastically about how what had previously looked impossible has begun to look possible

ENABLING LOVE TO CONQUER FEAR

FEAR CAN EAT us up. A strong sense of love and support upholds individuals and helps to cast out fear.

The idea

There is a biblical phrase, 'perfect love castes out fear'. 'Perfect love' is about supporting and upholding someone, respecting their integrity and enabling them to be the best person they can be. Love is about cherishing someone recognising their imperfections as well as their best qualities. Love is about forgiving someone and enabling them to learn from experience and become an effective influence for good with a range of different people.

Fear gets in the way of effective dialogue and using creative energies effectively. Fear stiffens us up and locks up our creative, open characteristics. Fear makes us run away from problems rather than address them. It saps energy and kills off initiative.

The leader as coach is enabling their people to be honest about their fears and be able to address them with reasonable equanimity. When fear can be named and defined it can potentially be boxed. Fear can be held at a distance and recognised as a distortion of reality.

The manager as coach is encouraging someone to recognise who they are supported and cherished by, and with whom there is a quality of relationship that will enable them to do difficult things well, knowing they have the support of others. Growing in maturity means somebody recognising the depth of support they receive from others and being able to reciprocate it.

The good leader as coach will enable an individual to handle their fears better and to recognise, appreciate and apply the support and encouragement they receive from others in a way that helps drive out the fear.

Sandra could become fearful of the reaction she might receive from different clients. She did not like criticism and was afraid of receiving it. Helen sought to persuade Sandra that the fear was irrational as the clients Sandra worked with respected her contribution. There was a level of trust and respect there which Sandra did not always allow herself to recognise. The consistent message from Helen to Sandra was to name her fears, box them and be open to believing that they were untrue. At the same time, Helen encouraged Sandra to build ever stronger relationships with her clients so that the sense of mutual support became stronger.

In practice

- Encourage individuals to name their fears

- Have open dialogue with people about their fears and how they might best be handled

- Believe that fear is reduced through establishing quality working relationships that are open and supportive

- Recognise the importance of individuals being upheld by the love of their wider circle of family and friends

- Demonstrate that you cherish those people you work with, recognising that that your support will help them diminish their fears

BOOKS BY DR PETER SHAW

Mirroring Jesus as Leader. Cambridge: Grove, 2004.

Conversation Matters: How to Engage Effectively with One Another. London: Continuum, 2005.

The Four Vs of Leadership: Vision, Values, Value-added, and Vitality. Chichester: Capstone, 2006.

Finding YourFuture: The Second Time Around. London: Darton, Longman and Todd, 2006.

Business Coaching: Achieving Practical Results Through Effective Engagement. Chichester: Capstone, 2007 (co-authored with Robin Linnecar).

Making Difficult Decisions: How to be Decisive and Get the Business Done. Chichester: Capstone, 2008.

Deciding Well: A Christian Perspective on Making Decisions as a Leader. Vancouver: Regent College Publishing, 2009.

Raise Your Game: How to Succeed at Work. Chichester: Capstone, 2009.

Effective Christian Leaders in the Global Workplace. Colorado Springs: Authentic/Paternoster, 2010.

Defining Moments: Navigating Through Business and Organisational Life. Basingstoke: Palgrave/Macmillan, 2010.

The Reflective Leader: Standing Still to Move Forward. Norwich: Canterbury Press, 2011 (Co-authored with Alan Smith).

Thriving in Your Work: How to be Motivated and Do Well in Challenging Times. London: Marshall Cavendish, 2011.

Getting the Balance Right: Leading and Managing Well.
London: Marshall Cavendish, 2012.

Leading in Demanding Times. Cambridge: Grove, 2013
(Co-authored with Graham Shaw).

The Emerging Leader: Stepping Up in Leadership.
Norwich: Canterbury Press, 2013 (Co-authored with Colin Shaw).

100 Great Personal Impact Ideas. London: Marshall Cavendish, 2013.

100 Great Coaching Ideas. London: Marshall Cavendish, 2014.

Celebrating Your Senses. Delhi: SPCK, 2014.

FORTHCOMING BOOKS

Sustaining Leadership. Norwich: Canterbury Press, 2014.

Wake Up and Dream. Norwich: Canterbury Press, 2015.

Effective Leadership Teams: A Christian perspective. London: Darton, Longman and Todd, 2015 (co-authored with Judy Hirst).

ABOUT THE AUTHOR

Dr Peter Shaw works with individuals, teams and groups to help them grow their strengths and tackle demanding issues confidently. His objective is to help individuals clarify the vision of who they want to be, the values that are driving them, the added value they want to bring and their sources of vitality.

His work on how leaders step up successfully into demanding leadership roles and sustain that success was recognised with the award of a Doctorate by Publication from Chester University in 2011.

Peter's clients enjoy frank, challenging conversations that lead to fresh thinking and new insights. It is the dynamic nature of the conversations that provide a stimulus for creative reflection and new action. He is often working with Chief Executives and Board members taking on new roles and leading major organisational change.

Peter has worked with Chief Executives and senior leaders in a range of different sectors and countries. He has led workshops on themes such as "Riding the Rapids", "Seizing the Future", "Thriving in your Work" and "Building Resilience", across five continents.

Peter has held a wide range of Board posts covering finance, personnel, policy, communications and delivery. He worked in five UK Government departments (Treasury, Education, Employment, Environment and Transport). He delivered major national changes such as radically different pay arrangements for teachers, a huge expansion in nursery education and employment initiatives which helped bring unemployment below a million.

He led the work on the merger of the UK Government Departments of Education and Employment. As Finance Director he managed a £40 billion budget and introduced radical changes in funding and accountability arrangements. In three Director General posts he led strategic development and implementation in major policy areas.

Peter has written a sequence of influential leadership books. He is a Visiting Professor of Leadership Development at Newcastle University Business School and a Visiting Professor at the University of Chester Business Faculty. He has worked with senior staff at Brighton University and postgraduate students at Warwick University Business School and at Regent College in Vancouver. He was awarded a CB by the Queen in 2000 for his contribution to public service.

Peter is a Reader (licensed lay minister) in the Anglian church and has worked with senior church leaders in the UK and North America. His inspiration comes from long distance walks: he has completed 14 long distances walks in the UK, including the St Cuthbert's Way, the South Downs Way, the Yorkshire Wolds Way, Cheshire Sandstone Trail and the Great Glen Way. Peter and his wife, Frances, have three grown up children who are all married. They have two grandchildren.